COOKING FOR
CHRISTMAS

COOKING FOR
CHRISTMAS

- FESTIVE FOOD FOR THE WHOLE HOLIDAY SEASON WITH OVER 200 BEST-EVER RECIPES
- INCLUDES CHECKLISTS, COUNTDOWNS AND MEAL PLANNERS TO ENSURE SUCCESS

EDITOR: MARTHA DAY

LORENZ BOOKS

This edition is published by Lorenz Books

Lorenz Books is an imprint of Anness Publishing Ltd, Hermes House, 88–89 Blackfriars Road, London SE1 8HA
tel. 020 7401 2077; fax 020 7633 9499; www.lorenzbooks.com; info@anness.com

© Anness Publishing Ltd 1997, 2005

UK agent: The Manning Partnership Ltd, 6 The Old Dairy, Melcombe Road, Bath BA2 3LR
tel. 01225 478444; fax 01225 478440; sales@manning-partnership.co.uk

UK distributor: Grantham Book Services Ltd, Isaac Newton Way, Alma Park Industrial Estate, Grantham, Lincs NG31 9SD
tel. 01476 541080; fax 01476 541061; orders@gbs.tbs-ltd.co.uk

North American agent/distributor: National Book Network, 4501 Forbes Boulevard, Suite 200, Lanham, MD 20706
tel. 301 459 3366; fax 301 429 5746; www.nbnbooks.com

Australian agent/distributor: Pan Macmillan Australia
Level 18, St Martins Tower, 31 Market St, Sydney, NSW 2000
tel. 1300 135 113; fax 1300 135 103; customer.service@macmillan.com.au

New Zealand agent/distributor: David Bateman Ltd, 30 Tarndale Grove, Off Bush Road, Albany, Auckland
tel. (09) 415 7664; fax (09) 415 8892

A CIP catalogue record for this book is available from the British Library.

Publisher: Joanna Lorenz
Project Editor: Sarah Ainley
Photography: Karl Adamson, Steve Baxter, James Duncan, Michelle Garrett, Amanda Heywood, Don Last & Patrick McLeavey
Recipes: Carla Capalbo, Jacqueline Clark, Carole Clements, Roz Denny, Nicola Diggins, Joanna Farrow, Christine France, Silvana Franco,
Christine Ingram, Judy Jackson, Elizabeth Lambert Oritz, Wendy Lee, Jane Stevenson, Laura Washburn,
Pamela Westland, Steven Wheeler & Elizabeth Wolf-Cohen
Designer: Siân Keogh

Previously published as *The Ultimate Christmas Cookbook*

1 3 5 7 9 10 8 6 4 2

For all recipes, quantities are given in both metric and imperial measurements,
and, where appropriate, measures are also given in standard cups and spoons.
Follow one set but not a mixture because they are not interchangeable.

 # $\mathscr{C}$ONTENTS

Introduction 6

Festive Starters 14

Main Dinners 34

Vegetarian Dishes & Vegetables 60

Buffet Dishes 92

Party Foods 118

Stuffings, Sauces & Preserves 138

Puddings & Desserts 158

Christmas Baking 194

Christmas Treats & Edible Gifts 220

Festive Drinks & Cocktails 240

Suggested Menus 252

Index 254

INTRODUCTION

Christmas is the time for high spirit and good cheer, a time for giving and for sharing. Food plays an essential part in the festive season: the gathering of friends and family around a table laden with rich and lavish fare somehow goes hand-in-hand with our idea of what Christmas is all about.

While all cooks know the importance of good food at Christmas, they also know that great demands will be made on their time. The secret of a carefree Christmas lies in the planning. Thinking ahead and preparing in advance mean that decision-making under pressure is avoided. As the holidays get closer, the list of things to do gets longer: planning meals and menus, shopping for the freshest and choicest ingredients, followed by all the necessary roasting, chopping, kneading and baking. The preparation of Christmas foods is as much a part of Christmas as the eating and can be just as much fun: include the whole family by delegating tasks. The excitement mounts as each task is crossed off the list.

This book is packed with inspirational ideas and valuable advice to take the cook smoothly through the festive season. There are over 200 recipes to choose from, including all the traditional favourites, plus a range of tempting alternative dishes which are every bit as festive as the customary fare. The introductory section includes a feature on setting the Christmas scene around the home with beautiful organic decorations. A count-down to Christmas will help you plan your time effectively so that you can ease yourself gently into the holiday season, plus there are professional tips for essential basic techniques such as roasting the turkey, lining a cake tin, and making almond paste and royal icing. A selection of sample menus for the main meal-time events completes the collection and will ensure that this Christmas is a happy and memorable one for the cook and the whole family.

Right: Natural decorations are by far the most beautiful.
This easily-made garland can be placed on
a mantelpiece or used as a door wreath.

Setting the Scene

Evergreen Garland

An evergreen garland, bringing together a host of natural materials, mirrors the beauty of the winter forest.

MATERIALS

*tape measure • wire-mesh netting •
wire cutters • absorbent stem-holding
foam, soaked in water • knife • scissors
• secateurs • stub wires • selection of
evergreens such as pine, holly, ivy,
cypress • bare twigs such as apple and
teasels • dried ferns, sprayed gold
(optional) • large pine cones •
selection of baubles and ribbons*

1 Measure the length of the fireplace
or doorway to be decorated. Cut the
appropriate length of wire-mesh netting
and trim it to a width of 25cm/10in,
using wire cutters. Cut blocks of
absorbent foam into 6 pieces and place
them end to end along the centre of the
netting. Fold over the netting to secure
the foam blocks, and twist the cut edges
together. Measure and mark the centre
of the garland length.

2 Decorate the garland with the
evergreens and natural materials,
pushing the stems under the wire
mesh and into the foam. Continue
adding materials until you reach the end
of the wire cone. Return to the centre of
the garland and decorate outwards in
the opposite direction.

3 Twist the stub wires around a few
pine cones and push the wires into the
foam at intervals along the garland.

4 Twist the wires around the garland to
hang it securely. Decorate with a ribbon
bow, baubles or large pine cones.

Twig Heart Door Wreath

Welcome seasonal guests with a door wreath that is charming in its simplicity.

MATERIALS

*garden shears • pliable branches
such as Buddleia, cut from the garden
• ruler • florist's wire • sea-grass string
• variegated trailing ivy • red berries •
tree ivy • white rose • golden twine*

1 Use garden shears to cut 6 lengths
of pliable branches, 72cm/28in long.
Wire three branches together at one
end. Repeat with the other three. Cross
the two bundles over at the wired end,
then wire them together in the crossed-
over position.

2 Holding the crossed, wired ends,
ease the long end round and down.
Repeat with the other side to form a
heart shape. Wire the bottom end.

3 Bind the wiring with sea-grass
string and make a hanging loop.

4 Entwine ivy around the heart shape.
Add berries. Make a posy of tree-ivy
leaves and a white rose and tie it with
golden twine. Wire the posy at the top
of the heart shape.

Everlasting Christmas Tree

This delightful little tree, made from dyed, preserved oak leaves and decorated with gilded cones makes an enchanting Christmas decoration. Group several together to make a table centrepiece.

MATERIALS

bunch of dried, dark oak leaves • florist's wire • small pine cones • picture framer's wax gilt • flowerpot, 18cm/7in tall • small, dry florist's foam cone • knife • 4 florist's stub wires • large , dry florist's foam, 18cm/7in tall

1 Wire up bunches of about four leaves, making separate bunches of large, medium and small leaves.

2 Insert wires into the bottom end of each pine cone and twist the ends together. Gild each cone by rubbing on wax gilt.

3 Prepare the pot by cutting the smaller foam cone to fit, adding stub wires and positioning the larger cone onto this. Attach the leaves, starting at the top and working down, to make a realistic shape. Add the gilded cones.

Advent Candle Ring

An advent ring makes a pretty centrepiece. This one uses cinnamon sticks for a rich sensual aroma.

MATERIALS

florist's foam • knife • florist's ring basket • 4 church candles • moss • dried orange slices • florist's stub wires • garden shears • cinnamon sticks • golden twine • tree ivy • Cape gooseberries

1 Soak the foam and cut it to fit the ring basket. Position the church candles in the foam, then cover the florist's foam with moss, pushing it well down at the sides of the basket.

2 Pass stub wire through the centre of the orange slices and twist the ends.

3 Wire the cinnamon sticks into bundles, then tie them with golden twine and pass a wire through the string. Wire the ivy leaves into bundles.

4 Position the ivy leaves into the ring. Decorate with orange slices and cinnamon sticks, placing the gooseberries on the candle ring, at intervals.

COUNT-DOWN TO CHRISTMAS

This at-a-glance timetable will help you plan and organize your Christmas cooking.

If you have chosen your menu from one of those suggested at the back of the book,

the table below suggests when the components may be prepared.

LATE AUTUMN
Make a selection of preserves and relishes such as Crab-apple & Lavender Jelly or Christmas Chutney, to serve with cold meats and pies.

NOVEMBER
Second week
Make Moist and Rich Christmas Cake.

Third week
Feed Moist and Rich Christmas Cake.

Fourth week
Make Traditional Christmas Pudding. Plan the Christmas Dinner: consider the number of guests and their food preferences before you plan the menu. Order turkey, goose, beef or ham. Continue to feed Moist and Rich Christmas Cake.

DECEMBER
First week
Make Light Jewelled Fruit Cake. Make mincemeat for De Luxe Mincemeat Tart. Continue to feed Moist and Rich Christmas Cake. Compile complete shopping list for main Christmas meals under headings for different stores or for the various counters at the supermarket.

Second week
Make Almond Paste to cover Moist and Rich Christmas Cake. Shop for dry goods such as rice, dried fruits and flour. Order special bread requirements. Order milk, cream and other dairy produce. Make Cumberland Rum Butter.

Third week
Make Roquefort Tartlets and other pastry-type cocktail savouries and freeze them. Cover Moist and Rich Christmas Cake with royal icing, leave one day, then cover and store.

Fourth week
Shop for chilled ingredients. Buy wines and other drinks.

21 DECEMBER
Check thawing time for frozen turkey, duck, beef or other meat. Large turkeys (11.5kg/25lb) need 86 hours (3½ days) to thaw in the refrigerator, or 40 hours at room temperature. Make a note to take the meat from the freezer at the appropriate time.

23 DECEMBER
Shop for fresh vegetables, if not possible to do so on 24 December. Make Cheese and Spinach Flan and freeze if not making on Christmas Day. Make Crunchy Apple and Almond Flan.

24 DECEMBER
Shop for fresh vegetables, if possible. Assemble Christmas Salad and refrigerate dressing separately. Make stuffing for poultry. Cook poultry giblets to make gravy. Defrost cocktail pastries. Prepare bacon rolls by threading them on to cocktail sticks.

Left: Pottery moulds were often used in Victorian times to give variety to the shape of the Christmas pudding.

CHRISTMAS DAY

This timetable is planned for Christmas Dinner to be served at 2.00pm.

If you wish to serve it at a different time, please adjust the times accordingly.

8.30AM Stuff the poultry. Make force-meat balls with any leftover stuffing, or spoon it into greased ovenproof dishes. Set the table.

9.00AM Put a steamer or large saucepan on the cooker and bring water to the boil. Put the Christmas Pudding on to steam.

TO COOK A 4.5KG/10LB TURKEY

9.05AM Set oven to 220°C/425°F/Gas 7.

9.25AM Put turkey in oven.

9.45AM Reduce heat to 180°C/350°F/ Gas 4.
 Baste turkey now and at frequent intervals.

12.15PM Put potatoes around meat. Remove foil from turkey and baste again.
 Turn the potatoes.

12.45PM Increase heat to 200°C/400°F/ Gas 6.
 Put any dishes of stuffing in oven.

1.45PM Remove turkey and potatoes from oven, put on heated dish, cover with foil and keep warm. Make gravy and grill bacon rolls.

TO COOK VEGETARIAN MENU

11.15AM Make pastry for Cheese and Spinach Flan, if not cooking from frozen. (If you are making Christmas Pie, begin 20 minutes earlier to allow time to chill the assembled pie.)

11.45AM Put pastry in the fridge and chill. Prepare sprouts for Festive Brussels Sprouts.

12.15PM Preheat oven for Cheese and Spinach Flan.
 Remove pastry from fridge and assemble. (For Christmas Pie, chill assembled dish for 20 minutes before baking. Preheat oven 10 minutes before removing pie from fridge.)

1.00PM Put flan or pie in oven.

1.20PM Simmer chestnuts for 10 minutes.

1.30PM Simmer sprouts for 5 minutes.

1.35PM Simmer carrots for 5 minutes.

1.40PM Gently reheat all vegetables together.

1.45PM Remove flan or pie from oven.

2.00PM Serve first course.

Above: Bundles of cinnamon sticks are tied together with ribbon for a scented tree trim. Fresh cranberries are threaded onto sewing thread and fixed to the ribbon, as a complement to the festive colours on the tree.

Basic Techniques

Carving a Turkey

1 First remove the leg by cutting the skin between the breast and leg. Press the leg flat, to expose the joint. Cut between the bones through the joint.

2 Cut the leg in two, through the joint.

3 Carve the leg into slices.

4 Remove the wing, cutting through the joint in the same way as for the leg.

5 Carve the breast in slices, starting at the front of the breast. Carve slices from the back of the breast, alternating the slices between front and back, until all the breast has been carved.

Times for Roasting Turkey

When choosing a turkey for Christmas, you should allow about 450g/1lb of dressed (plucked and oven-ready) bird per head. A good size turkey to buy for Christmas is 4.5kg/10lb. This will serve about 12 people, with leftovers for the following day.

Thaw a frozen turkey, still in its bag, on a plate at room temperature (18–21°C/65–70°F) until the legs are flexible and there are no ice crystals in the cavity of the bird. Remove the giblets from the cavity as soon as the bird has thawed enough.

Oven-ready weight	Thawing time	Number of servings	Cooking time
3.5kg/8lb	18 hours	8–10 people	2½–3½ hours
4.5kg/10lb	19 hours	12–14 people	3½–4 hours
5.5kg/12lb	20 hours	16–18 people	3¾–4½ hours
6.3kg/14lb	24 hours	18–20 people	4–5 hours

These times apply to a turkey weighed after stuffing and at room temperature. Cook in a moderate oven, 180°C/350°F/Gas 4, covered with butter and bacon rashers and loosely covered with foil.

To test whether the turkey is fully cooked, push a skewer into the thickest part of the leg and press the flesh; the juices should run clear and free of any blood. The legs take longer than the breast to cook; keep the breast covered with foil until the legs are cooked. The foil can be removed for the final hour of cooking, to brown and crisp the skin. The turkey should be basted with the juices from the roasting tin, every hour of cooking.

Plan for the turkey to be ready 15–20 minutes before you want to serve dinner. Remove it from the oven and allow the flesh to relax before carving it.

Almond Paste

Use almond paste as a base for royal or fondant icing. It will help to keep the cake moist.

Ingredients

350g/12oz/4 cups ground almonds
175g/6oz/⅞ cup caster sugar
175g/6oz/1½ cups icing sugar
5ml/1 tsp lemon juice
1.5ml/¼ tsp almond essence
1 egg

Makes enough to cover a
20cm/8in round cake

1 Sift the ground almonds, caster sugar and icing sugar together in a large mixing bowl.

2 Using a fork, beat the lemon juice, almond essence and egg together in a small bowl. Stir them into the dry ingredients in the mixing bowl until well blended.

3 Knead the paste together until smooth. Wrap in clear film until needed.

ROYAL ICING

INGREDIENTS

2 egg whites
5ml/1 tsp lemon juice
5ml/1 tsp glycerine (optional)
450g/1lb icing sugar

Makes enough to cover a
20cm/8in round cake

1 In a large bowl, beat the egg whites, lemon juice and glycerine (if using) together with a fork.

2 Sift in enough icing sugar to make a thick paste. Stir to mix.

3 Using a wooden spoon, beat in the remaining icing sugar until the icing forms stiff peaks. Cover with clear film until needed.

LINING A CAKE TIN

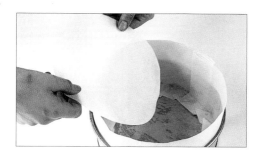

1 Place the cake tin on a double piece of greaseproof paper. Draw around the base of the tin and cut out two circles to fit inside the tin.

2 Measure the circumference of the tin with a piece of string and cut a double strip of greaseproof paper slightly longer than the circumference. Fold over 2.5cm/1in along one long side. Cut diagonal slits in the folded-over part, up to the fold line.

3 Grease the tin. Place one circle of paper in the base of the tin. Fit the double strip around the tin, neatly arranging the snipped edge over the bottom of the tin so it fits flat. Place the second circle of greaseproof paper on top, to make a smooth base.

FONDANT ICING

INGREDIENTS

60ml/4 tbsp water
15g/½oz/1 tbsp powdered gelatine
10ml/2 tsp liquid glucose
500g/1¼lb/5 cups icing sugar

Makes enough to cover a
20cm/8in round cake

1 Put the gelatine in the water in a small bowl and soak for 2 minutes. Place the bowl in a saucepan of hot water and leave to dissolve over a very gentle heat.

2 Remove the bowl from the hot water and add the glucose to the liquid.

3 Sift the icing sugar into a bowl and add the gelatine mixture. Mix and knead to a paste. Wrap the icing in clear film until needed.

Festive Starters

Christmas is all about anticipation: the people you will see, the gifts you will receive and, of course, the Christmas meals you eat together. A Christmas meal is like a good novel – a tempting starter that builds to an exciting middle and leads on to a satisfying ending. All of the festive starters in this chapter will tempt the senses, and the trick is to make a good match between the colours, textures and richness of all your courses. Virtually any will complement the traditional turkey, but keep in mind Pumpkin Soup for a beautiful colour contrast, or Oriental Duck Consommé for an exotic touch. Farmhouse Pâté will balance lighter fish or chicken lunches, while Grilled Brie and Walnuts or Roquefort Tartlets will suit beef or lamb dishes.

Carrot and Coriander Soup

Nearly all root vegetables make excellent soups as they purée well and have an earthy flavour which

complements the sharper flavours of herbs and spices. Carrots are particularly versatile, and

this simple soup is elegant in both flavour and appearance.

INGREDIENTS

450g/1lb carrots, preferably young and tender
15ml/1 tbsp sunflower oil
40g/1½oz/3 tbsp butter
1 onion, chopped
1 celery stick, plus 2–3 pale leafy celery tops
2 small potatoes, chopped
1 litre/1¾ pints/4 cups chicken stock
10–15ml/2–3 tsp ground coriander
15ml/1 tbsp chopped fresh coriander
200ml/7fl oz/⅞ cup milk
salt and freshly ground black pepper

Serves 4–6

1 Trim the carrots, peel if necessary and cut into chunks. Heat the oil and 25g/1oz/2 tbsp of the butter in a large flameproof, casserole or heavy-based saucepan and fry the onion over a gentle heat for 3–4 minutes until slightly softened, but not browned.

2 Cut the celery stick into slices. Add the celery and potatoes to the onion in the pan, cook for a few minutes and then add the carrots. Fry over a gentle heat for 3–4 minutes, stirring, and then cover. Reduce the heat and sweat for 10 minutes. Shake the pan occasionally so that the vegetables do not stick.

3 Add the stock, bring to the boil and then partially cover and simmer for a further 8–10 minutes until the carrots and potatoes are tender.

4 Remove 6–8 tiny celery leaves for use as a garnish and finely chop the remaining celery tops (about 15ml/ 1 tbsp once chopped). Melt the remaining butter in a small saucepan and fry the ground coriander for about 1 minute, stirring constantly.

5 Reduce the heat and add the finely chopped celery and fresh coriander and fry over a gentle heat for about 1 minute. Set aside.

6 Process the soup in a food processor or blender until smooth and pour into a clean saucepan. Stir in the milk, coriander mixture and seasoning. Heat gently, taste and adjust the seasoning as necessary. Serve the soup garnished with the reserved celery leaves.

COOK'S TIP

For a more piquant flavour, add a little lemon juice to the soup just before serving.

CREAM OF MUSHROOM SOUP

A good mushroom soup makes the most of the subtle and sometimes rather elusive flavour of mushrooms.

Button mushrooms are used here for their pale colour; chestnut or, better still, field mushrooms give

a fuller flavour but will turn the soup a darker shade of brown.

INGREDIENTS

275g/10oz/3¾ cups button mushrooms
15ml/1 tbsp sunflower oil
40g/1½oz/3 tbsp butter
1 small onion, finely chopped
15ml/1 tbsp plain flour
450ml/¾ pint/1¾ cups vegetable stock
450ml/¾ pint/1¾ cups milk
pinch of dried basil
30–45ml/2–3 tbsp single cream (optional)
fresh basil leaves, to garnish
salt and freshly ground black pepper

Serves 4

1 Pull the mushroom caps away from the stalks. Finely slice the caps and finely chop the stalks, keeping the two piles separate.

3 Stir in the flour and cook for about 1 minute. Gradually add the stock and milk to make a smooth, thin sauce. Add the basil, and season with salt and pepper. Bring to the boil and then simmer, partly covered, for 15 minutes.

4 Allow the soup to cool slightly and then pour into a food processor or blender and process until smooth. Melt the remaining butter in a heavy-based frying pan, and fry the remaining mushrooms over a gentle heat for 3–4 minutes until they are just tender.

5 Pour the soup into a large, clean saucepan and stir in the sliced mushrooms. Heat until very hot but not boiling and add salt and ground black pepper to taste. Add a little of the single cream, if using. Ladle the soup into 4 warmed bowls and serve the soup at once, sprinkled with the fresh basil leaves.

2 Heat the sunflower oil and half the butter in a heavy-based saucepan and add the chopped onion, mushroom stalks and ½–¾ of the sliced mushroom caps. Fry for about 1–2 minutes, stirring frequently, and then cover and sweat over a gentle heat for 6–7 minutes, stirring occasionally.

Pumpkin Soup

The sweet flavour of pumpkin is good in soups, teaming well with other more savoury

ingredients such as potatoes to make a warm and comforting dish.

INGREDIENTS

15ml/1 tbsp sunflower oil
25g/1oz/2 tbsp butter
1 large onion, sliced
675g/1½lb pumpkin, cut into large chunks
450g/1lb potatoes, sliced
600ml/1 pint/2½ cups vegetable stock
good pinch of nutmeg
5ml/1 tsp chopped fresh tarragon
600ml/1 pint/2½ cups milk
about 5–10ml/1–2 tsp lemon juice
salt and freshly ground black pepper

Serves 4–6

1 Heat the sunflower oil and butter in a frying pan and fry the onion for 4–5 minutes until softened. Stir frequently.

2 Transfer the onions to a saucepan and add the pumpkin and potato. Stir well, then cover with the lid and sweat over a low heat for about 10 minutes until the vegetables are almost tender. Stir the vegetables occasionally to prevent them from sticking to the pan.

3 Stir in the stock, nutmeg, tarragon and seasoning. Bring the liquid to the boil and then simmer for about 10 minutes until the vegetables are completely tender.

4 Allow the liquid to cool slightly away from the heat, then pour into a food processor or blender and process until smooth. Pour back into a clean saucepan and add the milk. Heat gently and then taste, adding the lemon juice and extra seasoning if necessary. Serve piping hot with crusty brown bread rolls.

COOK'S TIP

Pumpkins are readily available in supermarkets throughout the winter months. Other unusual vegetables, such as squashes, can also be used to make tempting Christmas soups.

Oriental Duck Consommé

Christmas need not be about just traditional European flavours. This soup is both light

and rich at the same time and has intriguing flavours of Southeast Asia.

INGREDIENTS

*1 duck carcass (raw or cooked), plus 2
legs or any giblets, trimmed of fat
1 large onion, unpeeled, with root end
trimmed
2 carrots, cut into 5cm/2in pieces
1 parsnip, cut into 5cm/2in pieces
1 leek, cut into 5cm/2in pieces
2–4 garlic cloves, crushed
2.5cm/1in piece fresh root ginger, peeled
and sliced
15ml/1 tbsp black peppercorns
4–6 thyme sprigs, or 5ml/1 tsp dried thyme
1 small bunch coriander (6–8 sprigs),
leaves and stems separated*

For the Garnish
*1 small carrot
1 small leek, halved lengthways
4–6 shiitake mushrooms, thinly sliced
soy sauce
2 spring onions, thinly sliced
watercress or shredded Chinese leaves
freshly ground black pepper*

Serves 4

1 Put the duck carcass, with the legs or giblets, the onion, carrots, parsnip, leek and garlic in a large saucepan or flameproof casserole. Add the ginger, peppercorns, thyme and coriander stems, cover with cold water and bring to the boil over a medium-high heat. Skim off any foam on the surface.

2 Reduce the heat and simmer gently for 1½–2 hours, then strain through a muslin-lined sieve into a bowl, discarding the bones and vegetables. Cool the stock and chill for several hours or overnight. Skim off any congealed fat and carefully blot the surface with kitchen paper to remove any traces of fat.

3 For the garnish, cut the carrot and leek into 5cm/2in pieces and then lengthways in thin slices. Stack and slice into thin julienne strips. Place in a saucepan with the mushrooms. Pour over the stock and add a few dashes of soy sauce and some pepper.

4 Bring to the boil over a medium heat, skimming off any foam that rises to the surface. Adjust the seasoning. Stir in the spring onions and watercress or Chinese leaves. Serve the consommé sprinkled with the coriander leaves.

Warm Prawn Salad with Spicy Marinade

Most of the ingredients for this salad can be prepared in advance, but wait until just before serving to cook the prawns and bacon. Spoon them over the salad and serve with hot herb and garlic bread.

INGREDIENTS

225g/8oz/2 cups large, cooked, shelled prawns
225g/8oz smoked streaky bacon, chopped
mixed lettuce leaves, washed and dried
30ml/2 tbsp snipped fresh chives

For the Lemon and Chilli Marinade
1 garlic clove, crushed
finely grated rind of 1 lemon
15ml/1 tbsp lemon juice
60ml/4 tbsp olive oil
1.5ml/¼ tsp chilli paste, or a large pinch dried ground chilli
15ml/1 tbsp light soy sauce
salt and freshly ground black pepper

Serves 8

1 In a glass bowl, mix the prawns with the garlic, lemon rind and juice, 45ml/3 tbsp oil, the chilli paste and soy sauce. Season with salt and pepper. Cover with clear film and leave to marinate for at least one hour.

2 Gently cook the bacon in the remaining oil until crisp. Drain well.

3 Tear the lettuce into bite-size pieces and arrange on plates.

4 Just before serving, put the prawns with their marinade into a frying pan, bring to the boil, add the bacon and cook for one minute. Spoon over the salad and sprinkle with snipped chives.

SMOKED SALMON SALAD

This recipe works equally well using smoked trout in place of salmon. The dressing can be made in advance and stored in the fridge until you are ready to eat.

INGREDIENTS

4 thin slices white bread
oil, for frying
paprika, for dusting
mixed lettuce leaves
25g/1oz Parmesan cheese
225g/8oz smoked salmon, thinly sliced
1 lemon, cut into wedges

For the Vinaigrette Dressing
90ml/6 tbsp olive oil
30ml/2 tbsp red wine vinegar
1 garlic clove, crushed
5ml/1 tsp Dijon mustard
5ml/1 tsp runny honey
15ml/1 tbsp chopped fresh parsley
2.5ml/½ tsp fresh thyme
10ml/2 tsp capers, chopped
salt and freshly ground black pepper

Serves 8

1 First make the dressing. Put all the ingredients into a screw-top jar and shake the jar well. Season to taste.

2 With a small star-shaped cutter, stamp out shapes from the bread. Heat 2.5cm/1in oil in a shallow frying pan until the oil is almost smoking (test it with a cube of bread: it should sizzle on the surface and brown within 30 seconds). Fry the croûtons in batches until golden brown. Remove the croûtons and drain on kitchen paper. Dust with paprika and leave to cool.

3 Wash the lettuce, dry the leaves and tear them into small bite-size pieces. Wrap the leaves in a clean, damp tea towel and keep the lettuce in the fridge until ready to serve.

4 Slice the Parmesan cheese into wafer-thin flakes with a vegetable peeler. Put the flakes into a dish and cover with clear film.

5 Cut the salmon into 1cm/½in strips no more than 5cm/2in long.

6 Arrange the lettuce on individual plates, scatter over the Parmesan flakes and arrange the salmon strips on top. Shake the dressing vigorously again and spoon over the salad. Scatter over the croûtons and place a lemon wedge on the side of each plate.

CHRISTMAS SALAD

A light and simple first course that can be prepared ahead and assembled just before serving.

INGREDIENTS

Mixed red and green lettuce leaves
2 sweet pink grapefruit
1 large or 2 small avocados, peeled and cubed

For the Dressing
90ml/6 tbsp light olive oil
30ml/2 tbsp red wine vinegar
1 garlic clove, crushed
5ml/1 tsp Dijon mustard
salt and freshly ground black pepper

For the Caramelized Orange Peel
4 oranges
50g/2oz/4 tbsp caster sugar
60ml/4 tbsp cold water

Serves 8

1 For the caramelized peel, using a vegetable peeler, remove the rind from the oranges in thin strips and reserve the fruit. Scrape away the white pith from the rind with a sharp knife, and cut the rind in fine shreds.

2 Put the sugar and water in a small pan and heat gently until the sugar has dissolved. Then add the shreds of orange rind, increase the heat and boil steadily for 5 minutes, until the rind is tender. Using two forks, remove the orange rind from the syrup and spread it out on a wire rack to dry. (This can be done the day before.) Reserve the syrup to add to the dressing.

3 Wash and dry the lettuce and tear the leaves into bite-size pieces. Wrap them in a damp tea towel and chill. Over a bowl, cut the oranges and grapefruit into segments, removing the pith.

4 Put the dressing ingredients into a screw-top jar and shake vigorously to emulsify the dressing. Add the reserved orange-flavoured syrup and adjust the seasoning to taste. Arrange the salad ingredients on individual plates with the avocados, spoon over the dressing and scatter on the caramelized peel.

Wild Mushroom Polenta

The wild mushrooms used here have a wonderful flavour and texture, which combine well

with polenta to make an unusual starter dish or light snack.

Ingredients

450g/1lb small new potatoes
1.3 litres/2¼ pints/5½ cups light vegetable stock
175g/6oz young carrots, trimmed and peeled
175g/6oz sugar snap peas
50g/2oz/4 tbsp unsalted butter
75g/3oz Caesar's mushrooms or hedgehog fungus, trimmed and sliced
5 horn of plenty fungus, fresh, chopped
250g/9oz/1½ cups fine polenta or cornmeal
2 shallots or 1 small onion, chopped
2 fist-size pieces of cauliflower fungus or 15g/½oz/¼ cup, dried
115g/4oz chicken of the woods, trimmed and sliced
150ml/¼ pint/⅔ cup single cream
3 egg yolks
10ml/2 tsp lemon juice
salt and cayenne pepper

Serves 4

1 Lightly oil a 23cm/9in loaf tin and line with a sheet of greaseproof paper. Set aside. Cover the potatoes with boiling water in a pan, add a pinch of salt and cook for 20 minutes. Bring the vegetable stock to the boil, add the carrots and peas and cook for 3–4 minutes. Remove the vegetables with a slotted spoon and keep warm. Add 25g/1oz/2 tbsp of the butter and all of the mushrooms to the stock and simmer for 5 minutes.

2 Introduce the polenta to the saucepan in a steady stream and stir for 2–3 minutes until thickened. Turn the polenta into the prepared tin, cover and allow to become firm.

3 For the sauce, melt the remaining butter, add the shallots or onion and cook gently. Add the cauliflower fungus, cut into bite-size pieces, with the chicken of the woods, and cook for 2–3 minutes. Add the cream and the reserved cooked vegetables and simmer to eliminate any moisture.

4 Remove from the heat, stir in the egg yolks and allow residual heat to slightly thicken the sauce. The sauce must not boil at this stage. Add the lemon juice, then season with salt and a dash of cayenne pepper.

5 To serve, turn the warm polenta out onto a board, slice with a wet knife and arrange on four warmed serving plates. Spoon the mushroom and vegetable sauce over the polenta. If preferred, the polenta loaf can be prepared in advance and stored in the freezer.

GOAT'S CHEESE SOUFFLÉ

Make sure everyone is seated before the soufflé comes out of the oven because it will begin to deflate almost

immediately. This recipe works equally well with strong blue cheeses such as Roquefort.

INGREDIENTS

25g/1oz/2 tbsp butter
25g/1oz/2 tbsp plain flour
175ml/6fl oz/¾ cup milk
1 bay leaf
freshly grated nutmeg
grated Parmesan cheese, for sprinkling
40g/1½oz herb and garlic soft cheese
150g/5oz firm goat's cheese, diced
6 egg whites, at room temperature
1.5ml/¼ tsp cream of tartar
salt and freshly ground black pepper

Serves 4–6

1 Melt the butter in a heavy saucepan. Add the flour and cook until golden, stirring. Pour in half the milk, stirring vigorously until smooth, then stir in the remaining milk and add the bay leaf. Season with a pinch of salt and plenty of pepper and nutmeg. Reduce the heat, cover and simmer for about 5 minutes, stirring occasionally.

2 Preheat the oven to 190°C/375°F/ Gas 5. Generously butter a 1.5 litre/ 2½ pint/6¼ cups soufflé dish and sprinkle with Parmesan cheese.

3 Remove the sauce from the heat and discard the bay leaf. Stir in both cheeses until melted.

4 In a clean, grease-free bowl, using an electric mixer or balloon whisk, beat the egg whites slowly until they become frothy. Add the cream of tartar, increase the speed and continue beating until they form soft peaks, then stiffer peaks.

5 Stir a spoonful of beaten egg white into the cheese sauce to lighten it, then pour the cheese sauce over the remaining whites. Using a metal spoon, gently fold the sauce into the whites until the mixtures are just combined, cutting down to the bottom, then along the side of the bowl and up to the top.

6 Gently pour the soufflé mixture into the prepared dish and bake for 25–30 minutes until puffed and golden brown. Serve at once.

GRILLED BRIE AND WALNUTS

This unusual cheese recipe will impress your guests as it looks as though it has been made

professionally. You'll be pleased to know that it requires almost no preparation.

INGREDIENTS

15g/½oz/1 tbsp butter, at room temperature
5ml/1 tsp Dijon mustard
675g/1½lb wheel of Brie or Camembert cheese
25g/1oz/¼ cup chopped walnuts
French stick, sliced and toasted to serve

Serves About 16–20

COOK'S TIP

A sharp serving knife will be appreciated by your guests as the grilled cheese will be quite sticky to cut.

2 Sprinkle the surface with the walnuts and grill for 2–3 minutes longer until the nuts are golden. Serve immediately with the French bread toasts. Allow your guests to help themselves as the whole grilled Brie makes an attractive centrepiece.

1 Preheat the grill. In a small bowl, cream together the butter and Dijon mustard, and spread evenly over the surface of the cheese. Transfer the cheese to a flameproof serving plate, and grill 12–15cm/4–6in from the heat for 3–4 minutes until the top just begins to bubble.

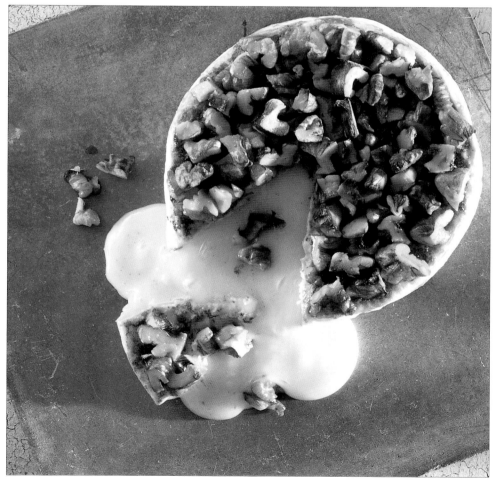

ROQUEFORT AND CUCUMBER MOUSSE

This refreshingly cool mousse makes a perfect starter to prepare ahead and store in

the fridge. If you prefer, other blue-veined French cheeses, such as Bleu d'Auvergne

or Fourme d'Ambert, may be used instead of Roquefort.

INGREDIENTS

18cm/7in piece cucumber
10ml/2 tsp powdered gelatine
75ml/5 tbsp cold water
100g/3½oz Roquefort cheese
200g/7oz full-, medium- or low-fat soft
cheese
45ml/3 tbsp crème fraîche or soured
cream
cayenne or white pepper
seedless red and green grapes and fresh
mint leaves, to garnish

Serves 6

1 Using a sharp kitchen knife, cut the cucumber lengthways into quarters. Remove the seeds and cut the cucumber strips into 2.5cm/1in pieces. Chop the cucumber pieces finely.

2 Sprinkle the gelatine over the cold water in a small heatproof bowl. Let the gelatine stand to soften for about 2 minutes, then place the bowl in a shallow pan of simmering water. Heat until the gelatine is dissolved, stirring occasionally.

3 In a mixing bowl (or in a food processor fitted with a metal blade) mix both types of cheese with the crème fraîche or cream until smooth. Add the dissolved gelatine and blend. Add the chopped cucumber to the bowl, mixing well without reducing the cucumber to a purée. Season to taste with cayenne or white pepper.

4 Rinse a 1.5 litre/2½ pint/6¼ cups dish or mould with cold water to prevent the mousse from sticking to the mould when turned out. Carefully spoon the mixture into the dish or mould and tap gently to remove air bubbles. Chill for 4–6 hours or overnight until well set.

5 To turn out, run a knife around the edge of the dish or mould, dip in hot water for 10–15 seconds and wipe the wet base. Place a large plate over the top of the dish and invert both together, shaking firmly to release the mousse. Garnish with the grapes and fresh mint leaves.

COOK'S TIP

The delicate taste and elegant appearance mean that this mousse would make a great addition to any buffet supper or party menu.

Foie Gras Pâté in Filo Cups

This is an extravagantly rich hors d'oeuvre so it is perfect for special occasions such as Christmas Day.

Any other fine liver pâté may be used if foie gras is unavailable.

INGREDIENTS

3–6 sheets fresh or defrosted filo pastry
40g/1½oz/3 tbsp butter, melted
225g/8oz tinned foie gras pâté or other
fine liver pâté, at room temperature
50g/2oz/4 tbsp butter, softened
30–45ml/2–3 tbsp Cognac or brandy
(optional)
chopped pistachios, to garnish

Makes about 24

COOK'S TIP

The pâté and pastry are best eaten soon after preparation. If preparing ahead and refrigerating, be sure to bring back to room temperature before serving.

1 Preheat the over to 200°C/400°F/ Gas 6. Grease a bun tray with 24 x 4cm/1½in cups. Stack the filo sheets on a work surface and cut into 6cm/ 2½in squares. Cover with a damp towel to prevent the pastry from drying out.

2 Keeping the rest of the filo squares covered, place one square on a work surface and brush lightly with melted butter, then turn over and brush the other side. Butter a second square and place it over the first at an angle. Butter a third square and place at a different angle over the first two sheets to form an uneven edge.

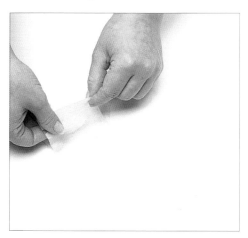

3 Press the pastry layers into the cups of the bun tray. Continue with the remaining pastry and butter until all the cups are filled.

4 Bake the filo cups for 4–6 minutes until crisp and golden, then remove and cool in the pan for 5 minutes. Carefully remove each filo cup to a wire rack and cool completely.

5 In a small bowl, beat the pâté with the softened butter until smooth and well blended. Add the Cognac or brandy to taste, if using. Spoon into a piping bag fitted with a medium star nozzle and pipe a swirl into each cup. Sprinkle with pistachio nuts. Refrigerate until ready to serve.

Chicken Liver Mousse

This mousse makes an elegant yet easy first course. The onion marmalade make a delicious

accompaniment, along with a salad of chicory or other bitter leaves.

INGREDIENTS

450g/1lb chicken livers
175g/6oz/³⁄₄ cup butter, diced
1 small onion, finely chopped
1 garlic clove, finely chopped
2.5ml/½ tsp dried thyme
30–45ml/2–3 tbsp brandy
salt and freshly ground black pepper
green salad, to serve

For the Onion Marmalade
25g/1oz/2 tbsp butter
450g/1lb red onions, thinly sliced
1 garlic clove, finely chopped
2.5ml/½ tsp dried thyme
30–45ml/2–3 tbsp red wine vinegar
15–30ml/1–2 tbsp clear honey
40g/1½oz/¼ cup sultanas

Serves 6–8

1 Use a sharp knife to trim the chicken livers, cutting off any green spots and removing any filaments or fat.

2 In a heavy-based frying pan, melt 25g/1oz/2 tbsp of the butter. Add the finely chopped onion and cook for 5–7 minutes over a gentle heat until soft and golden, then add the garlic to the pan and cook for 1 minute more. Increase the heat and add the chicken livers, thyme, salt and freshly ground black pepper. Cook for 3–5 minutes until the livers are coloured, stirring frequently; the livers should remain pink inside, but not raw. Add the brandy, stirring, and cook for a further minute.

3 Using a slotted spoon, transfer the livers to a food processor fitted with a metal blade. Pour in the cooking juices and process for 1 minute, or until smooth, scraping down the sides once. With the machine running, add the remaining butter, a few pieces at a time, until it is incorporated.

4 Press the mousse mixture through a fine sieve with a wooden spoon or rubber spatula until it has a creamy smooth consistency.

5 Line a 475ml/16fl oz/2 cup loaf tin with clear film, smoothing out as many wrinkles as possible. Pour the mousse mixture into the lined tin. Cool, then cover and chill until firm.

6 To make the onion marmalade, heat the butter in a frying pan, add the onions and cook for 20 minutes until softened and just coloured. Stir in the chopped garlic, thyme, vinegar, honey and sultanas and cook, covered, for 10–15 minutes, stirring occasionally, until the onions are completely soft and jam-like. Spoon into a serving bowl and allow to cool to room temperature.

7 To serve, dip the loaf tin into hot water for 5 seconds, wipe dry and invert. Lift off the tin, peel off the clear film and smooth the surface with a palette knife. Serve sliced, with the onion marmalade and a green salad.

FARMHOUSE PÂTÉ

This pâté is full of flavour and can be cut into slices for easy serving. You can make the pâté in

individual dishes or in a larger container, if you are expecting an unspecified number of guests.

INGREDIENTS

8 slices rindless streaky bacon
2 x 175g/6oz chicken breasts
225g/8oz chicken livers
1 onion, chopped
1 garlic clove, crushed
2.5ml/½ tsp salt
2.5ml/½ tsp freshly ground black pepper
5ml/1 tsp anchovy essence
5ml/1 tsp ground mace
15g/1 tbsp chopped fresh oregano
75g/3oz/1 cup fresh white breadcrumbs
1 egg
30ml/2 tbsp brandy
150ml/¼ pt/⅔ cup chicken stock
10ml/2 tsp gelatine

To Garnish
strips of pimento and black olives

Makes 450g/1lb

1 Preheat the oven to 160°C/325°F/ Gas 3. Press the bacon slices flat with a knife to stretch them slightly. Line the base and sides of each dish with bacon and neatly trim any excess off the edges.

2 Place the chicken breasts and livers, onion and garlic into a food processor. Process until smooth. Add the salt, pepper, anchovy essence, mace, oregano, breadcrumbs, egg and brandy. Process until smooth.

3 Divide the mixture between the dishes. Cover the dishes with a double thickness of foil and stand them in a roasting tin. Add enough hot water to come halfway up the sides of the tin.

4 Bake in the centre of the oven for 1 hour or until firm. Remove the foil to release the steam. Place a weight on top of each dish to flatten until cool.

5 Pour the juices from each dish into a measuring jug and make up to 150ml/ ¼ pint/⅔ cup with chicken stock. Heat in a pan until boiling. Blend the gela-tine with 30ml/2 tbsp water and pour into the stock, stirring. Allow to cool.

6 Garnish the pâté when cold, then spoon the gelatine mixture over the top. Chill until set. Cover with clear film.

BAKED EGGS WITH CREAMY LEEKS

This wonderful recipe can also be prepared using other vegetables, such as puréed spinach

or ratatouille, as a base. For such an elegant dish, it needs very little preparation time.

INGREDIENTS

*15g/½oz/1 tbsp butter, plus extra for
greasing
225g/½lb, about 2 cups, small leeks, thinly
sliced
75–90ml/5–6 tbsp whipping cream
freshly grated nutmeg
4 eggs
salt and freshly ground black pepper*

Serves 4

1 Preheat the oven to 190°C/375°F/ Gas 5. Generously butter the base and sides of four ramekins or individual soufflé dishes.

2 Melt the butter in a small frying pan and cook the leeks over a medium heat, stirring frequently, until softened but not browned.

3 Add 45ml/3 tbsp of the whipping cream and cook over a gentle heat for about 5 minutes until the leeks are very soft and the cream has thickened a little. Add plenty of salt, freshly ground black pepper and nutmeg to the frying pan, to season.

4 Arrange the ramekins or soufflé dishes in a small roasting tin and divide the leeks among them. Break an egg into each, spoon 5–10ml/1–2 tsp of the remaining cream over each egg and season lightly.

5 Pour boiling water into the baking dish to come halfway up the sides of the ramekins or soufflé dishes. Bake in the preheated oven for about 10 minutes, until the egg whites are set and the yolks are still quite soft, or a little longer if you prefer your eggs more well cooked.

ROQUEFORT TARTLETS

These can be made in shallow tartlet tins to serve hot as a first course. You could also make them

in tiny cocktail tins, to serve warm as bite-size snacks with a drink before a meal.

INGREDIENTS

175g/6oz/1½ cups plain flour
large pinch of salt
115g/4oz/½ cup butter
1 egg yolk
30ml/2 tbsp cold water

For the Filling
15g/½oz/1 tbsp butter
15g/½oz/1 tbsp flour
150ml/¼ pint/⅔ cup milk
115g/4oz Roquefort cheese, crumbled
150ml/¼ pint/⅔ cup double cream
2.5ml/½ tsp dried mixed herbs
3 egg yolks
salt and freshly ground black pepper

Makes 12

1 To make the pastry, sift the flour and salt into a large mixing bowl and rub the butter into the flour until it resembles breadcrumbs. Mix the egg yolk with the water and stir into the flour to make a soft dough. Knead until smooth, wrap in clear film and chill for 30 minutes.

2 Melt the butter, stir in the flour and then the milk. Boil to thicken, stirring continuously. Off the heat, beat in the cheese and season. Allow to cool. Bring the cream and herbs to the boil. Reduce the mixture to 30ml/2 tbsp. Beat into the sauce with the egg yolks.

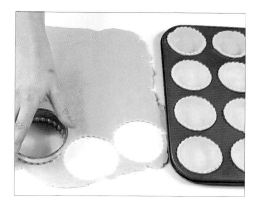

3 Preheat the oven to 190°C/375°F/ Gas 5. On a lightly floured work surface, roll out the pastry 3mm/⅛in thick. Stamp out rounds with a fluted cutter and use to line the tartlet tins.

4 Divide the filling between the tartlets so they are two-thirds full. Stamp out smaller fluted rounds or star shapes and lay on top of each tartlet. Bake for 20–25 minutes, or until golden brown.

Main Dinners

*F*or purists, there can be no other main course than Roast Turkey on Christmas Day, but an equally festive main dish of pheasant, goose or duck will provide such an attractive centrepiece that even traditionalists at the table won't object. And who's to say that the seasonal celebration can't be marked with a seafood alternative like Lobster Thermidor or Sea Bass with Citrus Fruit? Of course, venison, lamb or pork tenderloin all have their appeal, so the choice may be a difficult one. If you're having a big crowd for dinner, try adding together main dishes such as Roast Beef with Roasted Sweet Peppers or Chicken with Morels, and see which has less left over afterwards.

Roast Goose with Caramelized Apples

Choose a young goose with a pliable breast bone for the best possible flavour.

Ingredients

4.5–5.5kg/10–12lb goose, with giblets
(thawed overnight, if frozen)
salt and freshly ground black pepper

For the Apple and Nut Stuffing
225g/8oz/2 cups prunes
150ml/¼ pint/⅔ cup port or red wine
675g/1½lb cooking apples, peeled, cored
and cubed
1 large onion, chopped
4 celery sticks, sliced
15ml/1 tbsp mixed dried herbs
finely grated rind of 1 orange
goose liver, chopped
450g/1lb pork sausagemeat
115g/4oz/1 cup chopped pecans
2 eggs

For the Caramelized Apples
50g/2oz/4 tbsp butter
60ml/4 tbsp redcurrant jelly
30ml/2 tbsp red wine vinegar
8 small dessert apples, peeled and cored

For the Gravy
30ml/2 tbsp plain flour
600ml/1 pint/2½ cups giblet stock
juice of 1 orange

Serves 8

1 The day before you want to cook the goose, soak the prunes in the port or the red wine. After the soaking time, remove each prune from the marinade and stone each one and cut it into four pieces. Reserve the port or red wine and set aside.

2 The next day, mix the prunes with all the remaining stuffing ingredients and season well. Moisten with half the reserved port.

3 Preheat the oven to 200°C/400°F/ Gas 6. Stuff the neck-end of the goose, tucking the flap of the skin under and securing it with a small skewer. Remove the excess fat from the cavity and pack it with the stuffing. Tie the legs together to hold them in place.

4 Weigh the stuffed goose to calculate the cooking time: allow 15 minutes for each 450g/1lb. Put the bird on a rack in a roasting tin and rub the tin with salt. Prick the skin all over to help the fat run out. Roast for 30 minutes, then reduce the heat to 180°C/350°F/Gas 4 and roast for the remaining cooking time. Pour off any fat produced during cooking into a bowl. The goose is cooked if the juices run clear when the thickest part of the thigh is pierced with a skewer. Pour a little cold water over the breast to crisp the skin.

5 Meanwhile, prepare the apples. Melt the butter, redcurrant jelly and vinegar in a small roasting tin or a shallow ovenproof dish. Put in the apples, baste them well and cook in the oven for 15–20 minutes. Baste the apples halfway through the cooking time. Do not cover them or they will collapse.

6 Lift the goose onto the serving dish and let it stand for 15 minutes before carving. Pour off the excess fat from the roasting tin, leaving any sediment in the bottom. Stir in the flour, cook gently until brown, and then blend in the stock. Bring to the boil, add the remaining reserved port, orange juice and seasoning. Simmer for 2–3 minutes. Strain into a gravy boat. Surround the goose with the caramelized apples and spoon over the redcurrant glaze.

Roast Turkey

Serve this classic Christmas roast with stuffing balls, bacon rolls, roast potatoes, Brussels sprouts and gravy.

INGREDIENTS

*4.5kg/10lb oven-ready turkey, with giblets
(thawed, if frozen)
1 large onion, peeled and studded with
6 whole cloves
50g/2oz/4 tbsp butter, softened
10 chipolata sausages
salt and freshly ground black pepper*

*For the Stuffing
225g/8oz rindless streaky bacon, chopped
1 large onion, finely chopped
450g/1lb pork sausagemeat
25g/1oz/¹⁄₃ cup rolled oats
30ml/2 tbsp chopped fresh parsley
10ml/2 tsp dried mixed herbs
1 large egg, beaten
115g/4oz dried apricots, finely chopped*

*For the Gravy
25g/1oz/2 tbsp plain flour
450ml/¾ pint/1⅞ cups giblet stock*

Serves 8

1 Preheat the oven to 200°C/400°F/
Gas 6. Adjust the spacing of the shelves
to allow for the size of the turkey.
To make the stuffing, cook the bacon
and the chopped onion together over
a gentle heat in a heavy-based frying
pan until the bacon is crisp and the
onion is tender but not browned.
Transfer the cooked bacon and onion
to a large mixing bowl and add in all
the remaining stuffing ingredients.
Season well with plenty of salt and
freshly ground black pepper and mix
well to blend.

2 Stuff the neck end of the turkey
only, tucking the flap of skin under
and securing it with a small skewer
or stitching it in place with a thread.
Do not overstuff the turkey or the skin
will burst during cooking. Reserve any
remaining stuffing and set aside.

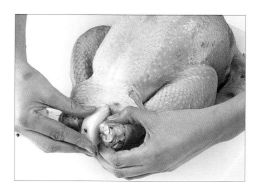

3 Put the onion studded with cloves
in the body cavity of the turkey and
tie the legs together with string to
hold them in place. Weigh the stuffed
bird and calculate the cooking time:
allow 15 minutes per 450g/1lb plus
15 minutes over. Place the turkey in
a large roasting tin.

4 Brush the turkey with the butter
and season well with salt and pepper.
Cover it loosely with foil and cook it
for 30 minutes. Baste the turkey with
the pan juices. Then lower the oven
temperature to 180°C/350°F/Gas 4
and cook for the remainder of the
calculated time. Baste the turkey
every 30 minutes or so.

5 With wet hands, shape the remaining
stuffing into small balls or pack it into a
greased ovenproof dish. Cook in the
oven for 20 minutes, or until golden
brown or crisp. About 20 minutes
before the end of cooking, put the
chipolata sausages into an ovenproof
dish and put them in the oven. Remove
the foil from the turkey for the last hour
of cooking and baste. The turkey is
cooked if the juices run clear when the
thickest part of the thigh is pierced with
a skewer.

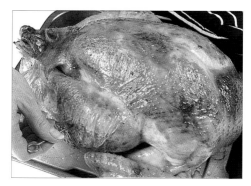

6 Transfer the turkey to a serving
plate, cover it with foil and let it stand
for 15 minutes before carving. To make
the gravy, spoon off the fat from the
roasting pan, leaving the meat juices.
Blend in the flour and cook for
2 minutes. Gradually stir in the stock
and bring to the boil. Check the
seasoning and pour into a sauce boat.
Remove the skewer and pour any juices
into the gravy. To serve, surround the
turkey with chipolata sausages, bacon
rolls and stuffing.

ROAST PHEASANT WITH PORT

Roasting the pheasant in foil helps to keep the flesh particularly moist and succulent. This recipe

is best for very young birds and, if you have a choice and an obliging butcher, you should

request the more tender female birds.

INGREDIENTS

vegetable oil
2 oven-ready hen pheasants
(about 675g/1½lb each)
50g/2oz/4 tbsp unsalted butter, softened
8 fresh thyme sprigs
2 bay leaves
6 streaky bacon rashers
15 ml/1 tbsp plain flour
175ml/6fl oz/¾ cup game or chicken stock
15ml/1 tbsp redcurrant jelly
45–60ml/3–4 tbsp port
freshly ground black pepper

Serves 4

1 Preheat the oven to 230°C/450°F/ Gas 8. Line a large roasting tin with a sheet of strong foil large enough to enclose both of the pheasants. Lightly brush the foil with vegetable oil.

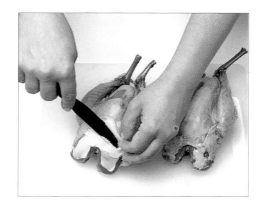

2 Wipe the pheasants with damp kitchen paper and remove any extra fat or skin. Using your fingertips, carefully loosen the skin of the breasts. With a round-bladed knife or small palette knife, spread the butter between the skin and the breast meat of each bird. Tie the legs securely with string then lay the thyme sprigs and a bay leaf over the breast of each bird.

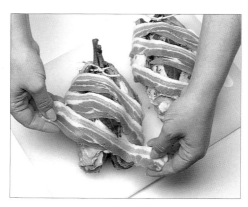

3 Lay bacon rashers over the breasts, place the birds in the foil-lined tin and season with plenty of ground black pepper. Bring together the long ends of the foil, fold over securely to enclose, then twist firmly together to seal.

4 Roast the birds for 20 minutes then reduce the oven temperature to 190°C/375°F/Gas 5 and cook for a further 40 minutes. Uncover the birds and roast 10–15 minutes more or until they are browned and the juices run clear when the thigh of each of the birds is pierced with a skewer. Transfer the birds to a board and leave to stand, covered with clean foil, for 10 minutes before carving.

5 Pour the juices from the foil into the roasting tin and skim off any fat. Sprinkle the flour in to the juices and cook over a medium heat, stirring continuously until the mixture is smooth. Whisk in the stock and the redcurrant jelly and bring to the boil. Simmer until the sauce thickens slightly, adding more stock if needed, then stir in the port and adjust the seasoning to taste. Strain the sauce and serve at once, with the pheasants.

VARIATION

Other game birds which would be suitable for this type of cooking include guinea fowl and partridge.

CHICKEN WITH RED WINE VINEGAR

These chicken breasts with their slightly tart taste are inspired by a famous French chef and make an original, light and tasty Christmas meal. You could substitute tarragon vinegar, if you prefer.

INGREDIENTS

*4 skinless boneless chicken breasts,
200g/7oz each
50g/2oz/4 tbsp unsalted butter
freshly ground black pepper
8–12 shallots, trimmed and halved
60ml/4 tbsp red wine vinegar
2 garlic cloves, finely chopped
60ml/4 tbsp dry white wine
120ml/4fl oz/½ cup chicken stock
15ml/1 tbsp chopped fresh parsley
green salad, to serve*

Serves 4

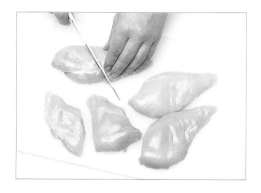

1 Using a sharp kitchen knife cut each chicken breast in half crossways to make eight pieces.

2 Melf half the butter in a heavy-based frying pan over a medium heat. Add the chicken and cook for 3–5 minutes until golden brown, turning once, then season with pepper.

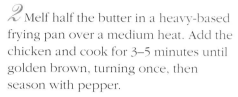

3 Add the shallot halves to the pan, cover and cook over a low heat for 5–7 minutes, shaking the pan and stirring the pieces occasionally.

4 Transfer the chicken pieces to a plate. Add the vinegar and cook, stirring frequently, for about 1 minute until the liquid is almost evaporated. Add the garlic, wine and stock and stir.

5 Return the chicken to the pan with any accumulated liquid. Cover and simmer for 2–3 minutes until the chicken is tender and the juices run clear when the meat is pierced with a knife or skewer.

6 Transfer the chicken and the shallots to a serving dish and cover to keep warm. Increase the heat and rapidly boil the cooking liquid until it has reduced by half.

7 Off the heat, gradually add the remaining butter, whisking until the sauce is slightly thickened and glossy. Stir in the parsley and pour the sauce over the chicken pieces and shallots. Serve at once with a green salad.

CHICKEN WITH MORELS

Morels are among the most tasty dried mushrooms and, although expensive, a little goes a long way.

Use fresh morels (about 275g/10oz), if you prefer, or chanterelles, shiitake or oyster mushrooms.

INGREDIENTS

40g/1½oz dried morel mushrooms
250ml/8fl oz/1 cup chicken stock
50g/2oz/4 tbsp butter
5 or 6 shallots, thinly sliced
100g/3½oz button mushrooms, sliced
1.5ml/¼ tsp dried thyme
175ml/6fl oz/¾ cup double cream
175ml/6fl oz/¾ cup brandy
4 skinless boneless chicken breasts about
200g/7oz each
15ml/1 tbsp vegetable oil
175ml/6fl oz/¾ cup Champagne or dry
sparkling white wine
salt and freshly ground black pepper

Serves 4

1 Put the morels in a strainer and rinse well under cold running water, shaking to remove as much sand as possible. Put them in a large heavy-based saucepan with the stock and bring to the boil over a medium-high heat. Remove the pan from the heat and leave to stand for 1 hour.

2 Remove the morels from the cooking liquid and strain the liquid through a very fine sieve or muslin-lined strainer and reserve for the sauce. Reserve a few whole morels and slice the rest.

3 Melt half the butter in a frying pan over a medium heat. Add the shallots and cook for 2 minutes until softened, then add the morels and mushrooms and cook, stirring frequently, for 2–3 minutes. Season well with salt and ground black pepper and add the thyme, 100ml/3½fl oz/⅓ cup of cream and the brandy. Reduce the heat and simmer 10–12 minutes until any liquid has evaporated, stirring occasionally. Remove the morel mixture from the frying pan and set aside.

4 Pull off the fillets from the chicken breasts. (The fillet is the finger-shaped piece on the underside of the breast.) Wrap the fillets tightly in clear film and freeze, to reserve for another use. Make a pocket in each chicken breast by cutting a slit with a sharp knife along the thicker edge, taking care not to cut all the way through the meat.

5 Using a small spoon, fill each pocket with one-quarter of the mushroom mixture, then close and, if necessary, secure with a cocktail stick to hold the stuffing inside the chicken.

6 Melt the remaining butter with the oil in a frying pan over a medium heat and cook the chicken breasts on one side for 6–8 minutes. Transfer to a plate. Add the Champagne or sparkling wine to the pan and boil to reduce by half. Add the strained morel cooking liquid and boil to reduce by half again.

7 Add the remaining cream and cook over a medium heat for 2–3 minutes until the sauce thickens and coats the back of a spoon. Season. Return the chicken to the pan with any juices and the reserved whole morels, and simmer for 3–5 minutes over a medium-low heat until the juices run clear when the meat is pierced with a skewer.

DUCK WITH ORANGE SAUCE

Commercially-raised ducks tend to have more fat than wild ducks. In this recipe, the initial slow cooking

and pricking the skin of the duck help to draw out the excess fat.

INGREDIENTS

2kg/4½lb duck
2 oranges
100g/3½oz/½ cup caster sugar
90ml/6 tbsp white wine vinegar or cider
vinegar
120ml/4fl oz/½ cup Grand Marnier or
orange liqueur
salt and freshly ground black pepper
watercress and orange slices, to garnish

Serves 2–3

1 Preheat the oven to 150°C/300°F/ Gas 2. Trim off all the excess fat and skin from the duck and prick the skin all over with a fork. Generously season the duck inside and out with salt and freshly ground black pepper, and tie the legs together with string to hold them in place.

2 Place the duck on a rack in a large roasting tin. Cover tightly with foil and cook in the preheated oven for 1½ hours. Using a vegetable peeler, remove the rind in wide strips from the oranges, then stack up two or three strips at a time and slice into very thin julienne strips. Squeeze the juice from the oranges and set it aside.

3 Place the caster sugar and vinegar in a small heavy-based saucepan and stir to dissolve the sugar. Boil over a high heat, without stirring, until the mixture is a rich caramel colour. Remove the pan from the heat and, standing well back, carefully add the freshly squeezed orange juice, pouring it down the side of the pan. Swirl the pan to blend, then bring back to the boil and add the orange rind and liqueur. Simmer for 2–3 minutes.

4 Remove the duck from the oven and pour off all the fat from the roasting tin. Raise the oven temperature to 200°C/ 400°F/Gas 6.

5 Roast the duck, uncovered, for 25–30 minutes, basting three or four times with the caramel mixture, until the duck is golden brown and the juices run clear when the thigh is pierced with a skewer.

6 Pour the juices from the cavity into the casserole and transfer the duck to a carving board. Cover loosely with foil and leave to stand for 10–15 minutes. Pour the roasting juices into the pan with the rest of the caramel mixture, skim off the fat and simmer gently. Serve the duck with the orange sauce, garnished with sprigs of watercress and orange slices.

ROAST LEG OF VENISON

The marinade for this recipe forms the base for a deliciously tangy, slightly sweet sauce which

complements perfectly the richness of roasted venison.

INGREDIENTS

1 onion, chopped
1 carrot, chopped
1 celery stick, chopped
3 or 4 garlic cloves, crushed
4–6 fresh parsley sprigs
4–6 fresh thyme sprigs
2 bay leaves
15ml/1 tbsp peppercorns, lightly crushed
750ml/1¼ pints/3 cups red wine
60ml/4 tbsp vegetable oil, plus more for brushing
1 young venison haunch, about 2.75kg/ 6lb, trimmed
30ml/2 tbsp plain flour
250ml/8fl oz/1 cup beef stock
1 unwaxed orange
1 unwaxed lemon
60ml/4 tbsp redcurrant or raspberry jelly
60ml/4 tbsp ruby port or Madeira
15ml/1 tbsp cornflour, blended with 30ml/2 tbsp water
15ml/1 tbsp red wine vinegar
fresh herbs, to garnish

Serves 6–8

1 Place the onion, carrot, celery, garlic, parsley, thyme, bay leaves, peppercorns, wine and oil in a dish large enough to hold the venison, then add the venison and turn to coat. Cover the dish with clear film and leave to marinate in the fridge for 2–3 days, turning occasionally.

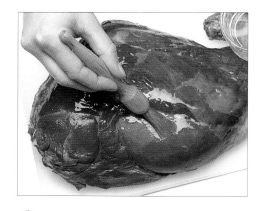

2 Preheat the oven to 180°C/350°F/ Gas 4. Remove the meat from its marinade and pour the marinade into a saucepan. Pat the meat dry, then brush with a little oil and wrap in foil.

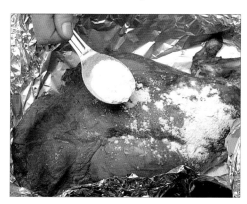

3 Roast the venison for 15–20 minutes per 450g/1lb for rare to medium meat. About 25 minutes before the end of the cooking time, remove the foil, sprinkle the venison with the flour and baste.

4 Add the stock to the marinade and boil until reduced by half, then strain and set aside.

5 Using a vegetable peeler, remove the rind from the orange and half the lemon. Cut the pieces into thin julienne strips. Bring a saucepan of water to the boil and add the orange and lemon strips. Simmer them for 5 minutes, then drain and rinse under cold water.

6 Squeeze the juice of the orange into a medium saucepan. Add the redcurrant or raspberry jelly and cook over a low heat until melted, then stir in the port or Madeira and the reduced marinade and simmer gently for 10 minutes, stirring.

7 Stir the blended cornflour mixture into the marinade and cook, stirring frequently, until the sauce is slightly thickened. Add the vinegar and the orange and lemon strips and simmer for a further 2–3 minutes. Keep warm, stirring occasionally, to keep the fruit strips separated.

8 Transfer the venison to a board and allow to stand, loosely covered with foil, for 10 minutes before carving. Garnish with your chosen fresh herbs and serve with the sauce.

FILET MIGNON WITH MUSHROOMS

This haute cuisine French dish was originally made with truffle slices but large mushroom caps

are less expensive and look just as attractive, especially when they are fluted.

INGREDIENTS

4 thin slices white bread
120g/4oz pâté de foie gras or mousse de foie gras
4 large mushroom caps
70g/2½oz/5 tbsp butter
10ml/2 tsp vegetable oil
4 fillet steaks, about 2.5cm/1in thick
45–60ml/3–4 tbsp Madeira or port
125ml/4fl oz/½ cup beef stock
watercress, to garnish

Serves 4

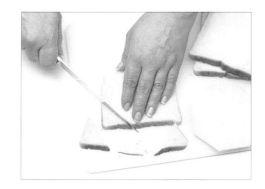

1 Cut the bread into rounds about the same diameter as the steaks, using a large round cutter or by cutting into squares, then cutting off the corners. Toast the bread and spread with the foie gras, dividing it evenly. Place the bread on warmed plates.

2 Flute the mushroom caps using the edge of a knife blade. Melt about 25g/1oz/1 tbsp of the butter and sauté the mushrooms until golden. Transfer the mushrooms to a plate and keep warm.

3 In the same pan, melt another 25g/1oz/1 tbsp of the butter with the oil, swirling to combine. When the butter just begins to brown, add the steaks and cook for 6–8 minutes, turning once, until cooked as preferred (medium-rare meat will still be slightly soft when pressed, medium will be springy and well-done firm). Place the steaks on the bread and top with the cooked mushroom caps.

4 Add the Madeira or port to the pan and boil for 20–30 seconds. Add the stock and boil until reduced by three-quarters. Swirl in the remaining butter. Pour a little sauce over each steak, then garnish with sprigs of watercress.

CHATEAUBRIAND WITH BÉARNAISE SAUCE

Chateaubriand is a lean and tender cut of beef from the thick centre of the fillet that is

pounded to give it its characteristic shape. This portion is usually served for two people and

would be perfect for a romantic Christmas meal for two.

INGREDIENTS

150g/5oz/⅔ cup butter, cut into pieces
25ml/1½ tbsp tarragon vinegar
25ml/1½ tbsp dry white wine
1 shallot, finely chopped
2 egg yolks
450g/1lb beef fillet, about 12.5–15cm/
5–6in long, cut from the thickest part of
the fillet
15ml/1 tbsp vegetable oil
salt and freshly ground black pepper
Sautéed Potatoes, to serve

Serves 2

1 Clarify the butter by melting in a saucepan over a low heat; do not boil. Skim off any foam and set aside.

2 Put the vinegar, wine and shallot in a small heavy saucepan over a high heat and boil to reduce until the liquid has almost evaporated. Remove from the heat and cool slightly. Add the egg yolks and whisk for 1 minute. Place the saucepan over a very low heat and whisk constantly until the yolk mixture begins to thicken and the whisk begins to leave tracks on the base of the pan, then remove the pan from the heat.

3 Whisk in the butter, slowly at first, then more quickly, until the sauce thickens. Season and keep warm.

4 Place the meat between two sheets of greaseproof paper or clear film and pound with the flat side of a meat pounder or roll with a rolling pin to flatten to about 4cm/1½in thick. Season with plenty of salt and pepper.

5 Heat the vegetable oil in a heavy-based frying pan over a medium-high heat. Add the meat and cook for about 10–12 minutes, turning once, until cooked as preferred (medium-rare meat will be slightly soft when pressed, medium will be springy and well-done will be firm).

6 Transfer the steak to a board and, using a very sharp kitchen knife, carve in thin, diagonal slices. If you prefer a smooth sauce, strain it through a fine sieve then serve with the steak, accompanied by Sautéed Potatoes.

Roast Beef with Roasted Sweet Peppers

This substantial and warming dish makes an ideal dinner for cold winter nights.

Ingredients

1.5kg/3–3½lb piece of sirloin
15ml/1 tbsp olive oil
450g/1lb small red peppers
115g/4oz/¾ cup mushrooms
175g/6oz thick-sliced pancetta, cubed
50g/2oz/2 tbsp plain flour
150ml/¼ pint/⅔ cup full-bodied red wine
300ml/½ pint/1¼ cups beef stock
30ml/2 tbsp Marsala
10ml/2 tsp mixed dried herbs
salt and freshly ground black pepper

Serves 8

1 Preheat the oven to 190°C/375°F/ Gas 5. Season the meat. Heat the oil in a pan, then brown the meat. Place in a roasting tin and cook for 1¼ hours.

2 Put the red peppers in the oven to roast for 20 minutes (or roast for 45 minutes if using larger peppers).

3 Near the end of the meat's cooking time, prepare the gravy. Roughly chop the mushroom caps and stems.

4 Heat the pan again and add the pancetta. Cook until the fat runs from the meat. Add the flour to the pan and cook for a few minutes until browned.

5 Stir in the red wine and stock and bring to the boil. Lower the heat and add the Marsala, herbs and seasoning.

6 Add the mushrooms and heat through. Remove the sirloin from the oven and leave to stand for 10 minutes. Serve with the peppers and hot gravy.

ROAST STUFFED LAMB

This lamb is stuffed with a tempting blend of kidneys, spinach and rice.

INGREDIENTS

*1.8–2kg/4–4½lb boneless leg or shoulder of
lamb (not tied)*
25g/1oz/2 tbsp butter, softened
15–30ml/1–2tbsp plain flour
120ml/4fl oz/½ cup white wine
250ml/8fl oz/1 cup chicken or beef stock
salt and freshly ground black pepper
watercress, to garnish
Sautéed Potatoes, to serve

For the Stuffing
65g/2½oz/5 tbsp butter
1 small onion, finely chopped
1 garlic clove, finely chopped
50g/2oz/⅓ cup long grain rice
150ml/¼ pint/⅔ cup chicken stock
2.5ml/½ tsp dried thyme
4 lamb kidneys, halved and cored
*275g/10oz young spinach leaves, well
washed*
salt and freshly ground black pepper

Serves 6–8

1 To make the stuffing, melt 25g/1oz/
2 tbsp of the butter in a saucepan over a
medium heat. Add the onion and cook
for 2–3 minutes until just softened, then
add the garlic and rice and cook for
about 1–2 minutes until the rice appears
translucent, stirring constantly. Add the
stock, salt and pepper and thyme and
bring to the boil, stirring occasionally,
then reduce the heat and cook for about
18 minutes, covered, until the rice is
tender and the liquid is absorbed. Tip
the rice into a bowl and fluff with a fork.

2 In a frying pan, melt 25g/1oz/2 tbsp
of the remaining butter over a medium-
high heat. Add the kidneys and cook for
2–3 minutes, turning once, until lightly
browned but still pink inside, then
transfer to a board and leave to cool. Cut
the kidneys into pieces and add to the
rice, season with salt and pepper and
toss to combine.

3 In a frying pan, heat the remaining
butter over a medium heat until
foaming. Add the spinach leaves and
cook for 1–2 minutes until wilted,
drain off excess liquid, then transfer
the leaves to a plate and leave to cool.

4 Preheat the oven to 190°C/375°F/
Gas 5. Lay the meat skin-side down on
a work surface and season with salt
and pepper. Spread the spinach leaves
in an even layer over the surface, then
spread the stuffing in an even layer
over the spinach. Roll up the meat like
a Swiss roll and use a skewer to close
the seam. Tie the meat at 2.5cm/1in
intervals to hold its shape, then place
in a roasting tin, spread with the
butter and season.

5 Roast for 1½–2 hours until the juices
run slightly pink when pierced with
a skewer, or until a meat thermometer
inserted into the thickest part of the
meat registers 57–60°C/135–140°F (for
medium-rare to medium). Transfer the
meat to a carving board, cover with foil
and leave for about 20 minutes.

6 Skim off the fat from the roasting tin.
Place the tin over a medium heat and
bring to the boil. Sprinkle over the flour
and cook for 3 minutes until browned,
stirring and scraping the base of the tin.
Whisk in the wine and stock and bring
to the boil. Cook for 5 minutes until the
sauce thickens. Season and strain.
Garnish the meat with watercress and
serve with the gravy and potatoes.

Baked Gammon with Cumberland Sauce

Serve this delicious cooked meat and sauce either hot or cold.

Ingredients

*2.25kg/5lb smoked or unsmoked gammon
joint
1 onion
1 carrot
1 celery stick
bouquet garni sachet
6 peppercorns*

For the Glaze
*whole cloves
50g/2oz/4 tbsp soft light brown or
demerara sugar
30ml/2 tbsp golden syrup
5ml/1 tsp English mustard powder*

For the Cumberland Sauce
*juice and shredded rind of 1 orange
30ml/2 tbsp lemon juice
120ml/4fl oz/½ cup port or red wine
60ml/4 tbsp redcurrant jelly*

Serves 8–10

1 Soak the gammon overnight in a cool place in enough cold water to cover. Discard this water. Put the joint into a large pan and cover it with more cold water. Bring the water to the boil slowly and skim off any scum that rises to the surface.

2 Add the vegetables and seasonings, cover the pan and simmer over a gentle heat for 2 hours.

3 Leave the meat to cool in the liquid for 30 minutes. Then remove it from the liquid and strip off the skin neatly with the help of a knife (use rubber gloves if the gammon is too hot).

4 Score the fat in diamonds with a sharp knife and stick a clove in the centre of each diamond.

5 Preheat the oven to 180°C/350°F/Gas 4. Put the sugar, golden syrup and mustard powder in a small pan and heat gently to melt them. Place the gammon in a roasting tin and spoon over the glaze. Bake it until golden brown, about 20 minutes. Put it under a hot grill, if necessary, to get a good colour. Allow to stand in a warm place for 15 minutes before carving.

6 For the sauce, put the orange and lemon juice into a pan with the port or red wine and jelly, and heat to melt the jelly. Pour boiling water on to the orange rind, drain, and add to the sauce. Cook for 2 minutes. Serve in a sauce boat.

TENDERLOIN OF PORK WRAPPED IN BACON

This easy-to-carve "joint" is served with an onion and prune gravy.

INGREDIENTS

*3 large pork fillets, weighing about
1.2kg/2½lb in total
225g/8oz rindless streaky bacon
25g/1oz/2 tbsp butter
150ml/¼ pint/⅔ cup red wine*

*For the Prune Stuffing
25g/1oz/2 tbsp butter
1 onion, very finely chopped
115g/4oz mushrooms, finely chopped
4 ready-to-eat prunes, stoned and chopped
10ml/2 tsp mixed dried herbs
115g/4oz/2 cups fresh white breadcrumbs
1 egg
salt and freshly ground black pepper*

*To Finish
16 ready-to-eat prunes
150ml/¼ pint/⅔ cup red wine
16 pickling onions
30ml/2 tbsp plain flour
300ml/½ pint/1¼ cups chicken stock*

Serves 8

3 Stretch each rasher of bacon with the back of a large knife.

4 Overlap the rashers across the meat. Cut lengths of string and lay them at 2cm/¾in intervals over the bacon. Cover with a piece of foil and hold in place, and roll the "joint" over. Fold the bacon rashers over the meat and tie the string to secure them in place. Roll the "joint" back on to the bacon joins and remove the foil.

5 Place in a roasting tin and spread the butter over the joint. Pour the wine around the meat and cook for 1¼ hours, basting occasionally with the liquid in the roasting tin, until evenly browned. Simmer the remaining prunes in the red wine until tender. Boil the onions in salted water for 10 minutes, or until just tender. Drain and add to the prunes.

6 Transfer the pork to a serving plate, remove the string, cover loosely with foil and leave to stand for 10–15 minutes, before carving into slices. Remove any fat from the roasting tin, add the flour to the sediment and juices and cook gently for 2–3 minutes. Then blend in the stock, bring to the boil and simmer for 5 minutes. Adjust the seasoning to taste. Strain the gravy on to the prunes and onions, reheat and serve in a sauce boat with a ladle.

1 Preheat the oven to 180°C/350°F/ Gas 4. Trim the fillets, removing any sinew and fat. Cut each fillet lengthways, three-quarters of the way through, open them out and flatten.

2 For the stuffing, melt the butter and cook the onion until tender, add the mushrooms and cook for 5 minutes. Transfer to a bowl and mix in the remaining stuffing ingredients. Spread the stuffing over two of the fillets and sandwich together with the third fillet.

Sea Bass with Citrus Fruit

Try this recipe using fresh sea bass for friends or family who would appreciate an alternative to meat or poultry at Christmas time; it would be an ideal choice for a New Year's Eve dinner. The delicate flavour of the fish is complemented perfectly by the citrus fruits and olive oil.

INGREDIENTS

1 small grapefruit
1 orange
1 lemon
1 sea bass, about 1.35kg/3lb, cleaned and scaled
6 fresh basil sprigs
plain flour, for dusting
45ml/3 tbsp olive oil
4–6 shallots, peeled and halved
60ml/4 tbsp dry white wine
15g/½oz/1 tbsp butter
salt and freshly ground black pepper
fresh dill, to garnish

Serves 6

1 With a vegetable peeler, remove the rind from the grapefruit, orange and lemon. Cut into julienne strips, cover and set aside. Peel off the white pith from the fruits and, working over a bowl to catch the juices, cut out the segments from the grapefruit and orange and set them aside for the garnish. Slice the lemon thickly.

2 Preheat the oven to 190°C/375°F/ Gas 5. Wipe the fish dry inside and out and season the cavity with salt and pepper. Make three diagonal slashes on each side. Reserve a few basil sprigs for the garnish and fill the cavity with the remaining basil, the lemon slices and half the julienne strips of citrus rind.

3 Dust the fish lightly with flour. In a roasting tin or flameproof casserole large enough to hold the fish, heat 30ml/2tbsp of the olive oil over a medium-high heat and cook the fish for about 1 minute until the skin just crisps and browns on one side. Add the halved shallots to the roasting tin.

4 Place the fish in the preheated oven and bake for about 15 minutes, then carefully turn the fish over and stir the shallots. Drizzle the fish with the remaining oil and bake for a further 10–15 minutes until the flesh is opaque throughout.

5 Carefully transfer the fish to a heated serving dish and remove and discard the cavity stuffing. Pour off any excess oil and add the wine and 30–45ml/ 2–3 tbsp of the fruit juices to the pan. Bring to the boil over a high heat, stirring. Stir in the remaining julienne strips of citrus rind and boil for 2–3 minutes, then whisk in the butter. Spoon the shallots and sauce around the fish and garnish with fresh dill and the reserved basil and grapefruit and orange segments.

VARIATION

When sea bass is not available, a whole grey mullet or large trout would make a good alternative.

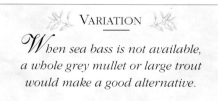

Sole with Prawns and Mussels

This luxurious dish is a classic seafood recipe. It is a true feast for fish lovers at any time

of the year and would make a welcome change at Christmas.

INGREDIENTS

75g/3oz/6 tbsp butter
8 shallots, finely chopped
300ml/½ pint/1¼ cups dry white wine
1kg/2¼lb mussels, scrubbed and
debearded
225g/8oz button mushrooms, quartered
250ml/8fl oz/1 cup fish stock
12 skinless lemon or Dover sole fillets,
about 75–150g/3–5oz each
30ml/2 tbsp plain flour
60ml/4 tbsp crème fraîche or double
cream
225g/8oz/2 cups cooked, peeled prawns
salt and white pepper
fresh parsley sprigs, to garnish

Serves 6

1 In a large heavy flameproof casserole, melt 15g/½oz/1 tbsp of the butter over a medium-high heat. Add half the shallots and cook for about 2 minutes until they are softened, but not browned. Stir the shallots frequently. Add the white wine and bring to the boil, then add the mussels and cover tightly. Cook the mussels over a high heat, shaking and tossing the pan occasionally, for 4–5 minutes until the shells open. Discard any mussels that do not open.

2 Transfer the mussels to a large bowl. Strain the mussel cooking liquid through a muslin-lined sieve and set aside. When cool enough to handle, reserve a few mussels in their shells for the garnish. Then remove the rest from their shells and set aside, covered.

3 Melt half the remaining butter in a large heavy-based frying pan over a medium heat. Add the remaining shallots and cook for 2 minutes until just softened, stirring frequently. Add the mushrooms and fish stock and bring just to simmering point. Season the fish fillets with salt and pepper. Fold or roll them and slide gently into the stock. Cover and poach for 5–7 minutes until the flesh is opaque. Transfer the fillets to a warmed serving dish and cover tightly to keep warm. Increase the heat and boil the liquid until it has reduced by one-third.

4 Melt the remaining butter in a small saucepan over a medium heat. Add the flour and cook for 1–2 minutes, stirring constantly; do not allow the flour mixture to brown. Gradually whisk in the reduced fish cooking liquid, the reserved mussel liquid and pour in any liquid from the fish, then bring to the boil, stirring constantly.

5 Reduce the heat to medium-low and cook the sauce for 5–7 minutes, stirring frequently. Whisk in the crème fraîche or double cream and keep stirring over a low heat until the sauce is well blended. Adjust the seasoning to taste, then add the reserved mussels and the cooked prawns to the sauce. Cook gently for 2–3 minutes to heat through, then spoon the sauce over the fish and serve garnished with fresh parsley sprigs and the mussels in their shells.

Lobster Thermidor

Lobster Thermidor is a rich and delicious dish that is luxurious enough

to serve at Christmas-time. Serve one lobster per person as a main course or

one filled shell each for a starter.

INGREDIENTS

2 live lobsters, about 675g/1½lb each
20g/¾oz/1½ tbsp butter
30ml/2 tbsp plain flour
30ml/2 tbsp brandy
120ml/4fl oz/½ cup milk
90ml/6 tbsp whipping cream
15ml/1 tbsp Dijon mustard
lemon juice, salt and white pepper
grated Parmesan cheese, for sprinkling
fresh parsley and dill, to garnish

Serves 2–4

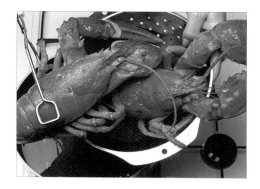

1 Boil the lobsters in a large saucepan of salted water for 8–10 minutes.

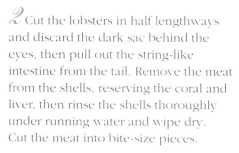

2 Cut the lobsters in half lengthways and discard the dark sac behind the eyes, then pull out the string-like intestine from the tail. Remove the meat from the shells, reserving the coral and liver, then rinse the shells thoroughly under running water and wipe dry. Cut the meat into bite-size pieces.

3 Melt the butter in a heavy saucepan over a medium-high heat. Stir in the flour and cook, stirring, until slightly golden. Pour in the brandy and milk, whisking vigorously until smooth, then whisk in the cream and mustard.

4 Push the lobster coral and liver through a sieve into the sauce and whisk briskly to blend. Reduce the heat to low and simmer gently for about 10 minutes, stirring frequently, until thickened. Season the sauce with salt, if needed, then add pepper and lemon juice.

5 Preheat the grill. Arrange the lobster shells in a gratin dish or shallow flameproof baking dish.

6 Stir the lobster meat into the sauce and divide the mixture evenly among the shells. Sprinkle with Parmesan cheese and grill until golden. Serve piping hot, garnished with fresh herbs.

SALMON STEAKS WITH SORREL SAUCE

Salmon and sorrel are a traditional combination – the sharp flavour of the sorrel balances the richness

of the fish. If sorrel is not available, use finely chopped watercress instead.

INGREDIENTS

2 salmon steaks (about 225g/8oz each)
5ml/1 tsp olive oil
15g/½oz/1 tbsp butter
2 shallots, finely chopped
45ml/3 tbsp whipping cream
100g/3½oz fresh sorrel leaves, washed and patted dry
salt and freshly ground black pepper
fresh sage, to garnish

Serves 2

1 Season the salmon steaks with salt and freshly ground black pepper. Brush a non-stick frying pan with oil.

2 Place the frying pan over a medium heat until hot. Add the salmon steaks and cook for about 5 minutes, until the flesh is opaque next to the bone. If you're not sure, pierce with the tip of a sharp knife; the juices should run clear.

3 Meanwhile, in a small saucepan, melt the butter over a medium heat and fry the shallots, stirring frequently, until just softened. Add the cream and the sorrel to the shallots and cook, stirring constantly, until the sorrel is completely wilted. Arrange the salmon steaks on two warmed plates, garnish with fresh sage and serve at once, with the sorrel sauce.

COOK'S TIP

If preferred, cook the salmon steaks in a microwave oven for about 4–5 minutes, tightly covered, or according to the manufacturer's guidelines.

Vegetarian Dishes & Vegetables

*I*n any Christmas celebration nowadays, it's likely that you'll have some vegetarian guests, and they'll appreciate more than just the leftover vegetables. Many recipes here, such as Vegetarian Christmas Pie or Cheese, Rice and Vegetable Strudel can stand alone as vegetarian main courses or can make a wonderful accompaniment to the turkey in place of traditional vegetables and potatoes. There is a strong ethnic element in vegetarian cooking, and Pumpkin Gnocchi or Spiced Vegetable Couscous will bring an international element to the Christmas table. And what would Christmas be without Brussels sprouts, parsnips and potatoes, all cooked in ways to make them extra special.

Vegetarian Christmas Pie

A sophisticated mushroom flan with a cheese-soufflé topping. Serve hot with cranberry relish

and Brussels sprouts with chestnuts and carrots.

INGREDIENTS

225g/8oz/2 cups plain flour
175g/6oz/¾ cup butter
10ml/2 tsp paprika
115g/4oz Parmesan cheese, grated
1 egg, beaten with 15ml/1 tbsp cold water
15ml/1 tbsp Dijon mustard

For the Filling
25g/1oz/2 tbsp butter
1 onion, finely chopped
1–2 garlic cloves, crushed
350g/12oz/5 cups mushrooms, chopped
10ml/2 tsp mixed dried herbs
15ml/1 tbsp chopped fresh parsley
50g/2oz/1 cup fresh white breadcrumbs
salt and freshly ground black pepper

For the Cheese Topping
25g/1oz/2 tbsp butter
25g/1oz/2 tbsp plain flour
300ml/½ pint/1¼ cups milk
25g/1oz Parmesan cheese, grated
75g/3oz Cheddar cheese, grated
1.5ml/¼ tsp English mustard powder
1 egg, separated

Serves 8

1 To make the pastry, sift the flour into a bowl and rub in the butter until the mixture resembles fine breadcrumbs. Stir in the paprika and the Parmesan cheese. Bind to a soft pliable dough with the egg and water. Knead until smooth, wrap in clear film and chill for 30 minutes.

2 For the filling, melt the butter and cook the onion until tender. Add the garlic and mushrooms and cook, uncovered, for 5 minutes, stirring occasionally. Increase the heat and drive off any liquid in the pan. Remove the pan from the heat and stir in the dried herbs, parsley, breadcrumbs and seasoning. Allow to cool.

3 Preheat the oven to 190°C/375°F/ Gas 5. Put a baking tray in the oven. On a lightly floured surface, roll out the pastry and use it to line a 23cm/ 9in loose-based flan tin, pressing the pastry well into the edges and making a narrow rim around the top edge. Chill for 20 minutes.

4 For the cheese topping, melt the butter in a pan, stir in the flour and cook for 2 minutes. Gradually blend in the milk. Bring to the boil to thicken and simmer for 2–3 minutes. Remove the pan from the heat and stir in the cheeses, mustard powder and egg yolk, and season well. Beat until smooth. Whisk the egg white until it holds soft peaks. Then, using a metal spoon, fold the egg white into the topping.

5 To assemble the pie, spread the Dijon mustard evenly over the base of the flan case with a palette knife. Spoon in the mushroom filling and level the surface by tapping the case firmly on the work surface.

6 Pour over the cheese topping and bake the pie on the hot baking tray for 35–45 minutes until the topping is set and golden. If you tap on the bottom of the flan case it should sound hollow. Serve at once or freeze until needed.

VEGETABLE GNOCCHI

This delicious vegetarian main course can be assembled well ahead of time – always a bonus at Christmas.

INGREDIENTS

450g/1lb frozen spinach
15g/½oz/1 tbsp butter
1.5ml /¼ tsp grated nutmeg
225g/8oz/1 cup ricotta or curd cheese
115g/4oz Parmesan cheese, grated
2 eggs, beaten
115g/4oz/1 cup plain flour
50g/2oz Cheddar cheese, grated
salt and freshly ground black pepper

For the Sauce
50g/2oz/4 tbsp butter
50g/2oz/4 tbsp plain flour
600ml/1 pint/2½ cups milk

For the Vegetable Layer
25g/1oz /2 tbsp butter
2 leeks or onions, sliced
4 carrots, sliced
4 celery sticks, sliced
4 courgettes, sliced

Serves 8

1 Put the spinach in a large saucepan with the butter and heat gently to defrost it. Using a wooden fork, carefully break up the spinach to help it thaw out, then increase the heat to drive off any moisture. Season well with salt, freshly ground black pepper and the grated nutmeg. Turn the spinach into a large bowl and mix in the ricotta or curd cheese, Parmesan cheese, eggs and flour. Beat the mixture well until it is smooth.

2 Shape the mixture into ovals with two dessert spoons and place them on a light floured tray. Chill for 30 minutes.

3 Have a large shallow pan of simmering, salted water ready. Cook the gnocchi in two batches, for about 5 minutes. As soon as the gnocchi rise to the surface, remove them with a slotted spoon and drain on a clean tea towel.

4 Preheat the oven to 180°C/350°F/ Gas 4. For the sauce, melt the butter in a pan, add the flour and blend in the milk. Boil until thickened and season.

5 For the vegetable layer, melt the butter and cook the leeks, carrots and celery. Add the courgettes, season and stir. Turn into a 2.4 litre/4 pint/ 10 cup ovenproof dish.

6 Place the drained gnocchi on top, spoon over the sauce and sprinkle with grated cheese. Bake for 30 minutes, until golden brown. Grill if necessary.

Vegetable Gougère

This makes a light vegetarian supper or a main meal served with baked potatoes.

INGREDIENTS

50g/2oz/4 tbsp butter
150ml/¼ pint/⅔ cup water
65g/2½oz/⅔ cup plain flour
2 eggs, beaten
1.5ml/¼ tsp English mustard powder
50g/2oz Gruyère or Cheddar cheese, cubed
salt and freshly ground black pepper
10ml/2 tsp chopped fresh parsley, to garnish

For the Filling
25g/1oz/2 tbsp butter
1 onion, sliced
1 garlic clove, crushed
225g/8oz/3 cups sliced mushrooms
15ml/1 tbsp plain flour
400g/14oz can tomatoes plus their juice
5ml/1 tsp caster sugar
225g/8oz courgettes, thickly sliced

For the Topping
15ml/1 tbsp grated Parmesan cheese
15ml/1 tbsp breadcrumbs, toasted

Serves 4

2 Beat the eggs into the paste. Season, add the mustard powder and fold in the cheese. Set aside.

3 For the filling, melt the butter and cook the onion. Add the garlic and mushrooms and cook for 3 minutes. Stir in the flour and tomatoes. Bring to the boil, stirring. Season with salt, pepper and sugar. Add the courgettes.

4 Butter a 1.2 litre/2 pint/5 cup ovenproof dish. Spoon the choux pastry in rough mounds around the sides of the dish and turn the filling into the centre. Sprinkle the Parmesan cheese and breadcrumbs on top of the filling. Bake for 35–40 minutes, until the pastry is well risen and golden brown. Sprinkle with chopped parsley and serve hot.

1 Preheat the oven to 200°C/400°F/ Gas 6. To make the choux pastry, melt the butter in a large pan, add the water and bring to the boil. As soon as the liquid is boiling, draw the pan away from the heat and beat in the flour all at once, and continue beating until a smooth, glossy paste is formed. Turn the paste into a large mixing bowl and set aside to allow to cool slightly.

CHEESE, RICE AND VEGETABLE STRUDEL

Based on a traditional Russian recipe called "Koulibiac", this dish makes a perfect vegetarian

main course or, for meat-eaters, a welcome accompaniment to cold leftover turkey or sliced ham.

INGREDIENTS

175g/6oz/⅞ cup long grain rice
25g/1oz/2 tbsp butter
1–2 leeks, thinly sliced
350g/12oz/5 cups mushrooms, sliced
225g/8oz Gruyère or Cheddar cheese, grated
225g/8oz feta cheese, cubed
30ml/2 tbsp currants
50g/2oz/½ cup chopped almonds or hazelnuts, toasted
30ml/2 tbsp chopped fresh parsley
275g/10oz packet frozen filo pastry, thawed
30ml/2 tbsp olive oil
salt and freshly ground black pepper

Serves 8

1 Cook the rice in boiling, salted water for 10–12 minutes, until tender but still with a little "bite". Drain, rinse under cold running water and set aside to drain again. Melt the butter and cook the leeks and mushrooms for 5 minutes more. Transfer to a large bowl and set aside until the vegetables have cooled.

2 Add the well-drained rice, the cheeses, currants, toasted almonds or hazelnuts, chopped fresh parsley and season to taste. (You may not need to add very much salt as the feta cheese is very salty.)

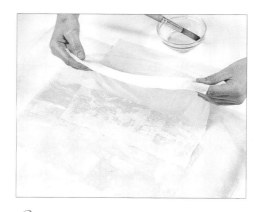

3 Preheat the oven to 190°C/375°F/Gas 5. Unwrap the filo pastry. Cover it with a piece of clear film and a clean damp cloth while you work to stop it drying out. Lay a sheet of filo pastry on a large piece of greaseproof paper and brush it with oil. Lay a second sheet on top, overlapping the first by 2.5cm/1in. Put another sheet with its long side running at right angles to the first two. Lay a fourth sheet in the same way, overlapping by 2.5cm/1in. Continue in this way, alternating the layers of two sheets so that the join between the two sheets runs in the opposite direction for each layer.

4 Place the filling mixture along the centre of the pastry sheet and carefully shape it with your hands into a rectangle that measures approximately 10 x 30cm/4 x 12in.

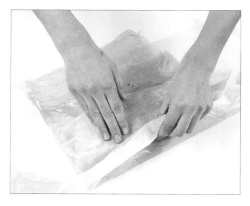

5 Fold the layers of filo pastry over the filling and carefully roll it over, with the help of the greaseproof paper, so that the join ends up being hidden on the underside of the strudel.

6 Lift the strudel on to a greased baking tray and gently tuck the edges under, so that the filling does not escape during cooking. Brush with oil and bake for 30–40 minutes, until golden-brown and crisp. Allow the strudel to stand for 5 minutes before cutting into thick slices. Serve at once or freeze until needed.

COOK'S TIP

The traditional Koulibiac dish has slices of hard-boiled egg as an ingredient in the filling – you could add it if you like.

VEGETABLE CRUMBLE WITH ANCHOVIES

The anchovies may be left out of this dish so that vegetarians can enjoy it, but they do give the vegetables a delicious flavour. Serve the dish on its own or as an accompaniment to sliced turkey or ham.

INGREDIENTS

450g/1lb potatoes
225g/8oz leeks
25g/1oz/2 tbsp butter
450g/1lb carrots, chopped
2 garlic cloves, crushed
225g/8oz/3 cups mushrooms, sliced
450g/1lb Brussels sprouts, sliced
40g/1½oz can anchovies, drained
salt and freshly ground black pepper

For the Cheese Crumble
50g/2oz/4 tbsp plain flour
50g/2oz/4 tbsp butter
50g/2oz/1 cup fresh breadcrumbs
50g/2oz Cheddar cheese, grated
30ml/2 tbsp chopped fresh parsley
5ml/1 tsp English mustard powder

Serves 8

2 Melt the butter and cook the leeks and carrots for 2–3 minutes. Add the garlic and sliced mushrooms and cook for a further 3 minutes. Add the Brussels sprouts. Season with pepper only, if using the anchovies, if not, add salt to taste. Transfer to a 2.5 litre/ 4 pint/10 cup ovenproof dish.

4 To make the crumble, sift the flour into a bowl and rub in the butter until the mixture resembles fine breadcrumbs, or process in a food processor. Add the breadcrumbs and fold in the grated cheese, and add the chopped fresh parsley and the mustard powder. Mix together well. Spoon over the vegetables and bake for 20–30 minutes until the crumble topping is golden and crispy.

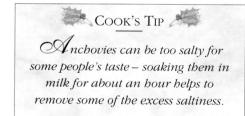

COOK'S TIP

Anchovies can be too salty for some people's taste – soaking them in milk for about an hour helps to remove some of the excess saltiness.

1 Peel and halve the potatoes and parboil them in salted water until just tender. Drain and cool. Cut the leeks in half lengthways and wash them thoroughly to remove any small pieces of grit or soil. Drain on kitchen paper and slice in 1cm/½in pieces.

3 Preheat the oven to 200°C/400°F/ Gas 6. Chop the anchovies and scatter them over the vegetables. Slice the cooked potatoes and arrange them on top of the anchovies.

CHEESE AND SPINACH FLAN

This flan freezes well and can be reheated. It makes an excellent addition to a festive buffet party.

INGREDIENTS

115g/4oz/½ cup butter
225g/8oz/2 cups plain flour
2.5ml/½ tsp English mustard powder
2.5ml/½ tsp paprika
large pinch of salt
115g/4oz/1 cup grated Cheddar cheese
45–60ml/3–4 tbsp cold water
1 egg, beaten, to glaze

For the Filling
450g/1lb frozen spinach
1 onion, chopped
pinch of grated nutmeg
225g/8oz/1 cup cottage cheese
2 large eggs
50g/2oz Parmesan cheese, grated
150ml/¼ pint/⅔ cup single cream
salt and freshly ground black pepper

Serves 8

1 Using your fingertips, rub the butter into the flour until it resembles fine breadcrumbs. Rub in the next four ingredients. Alternatively, process in a food processor. Bind to a dough with the cold water. Knead until smooth and pliable, wrap in clear film and chill for about 30 minutes.

2 Put the spinach and onion in a pan, cover, and cook slowly. Increase the heat to drive off any water. Season with salt, pepper and nutmeg. Turn the spinach into a bowl, cool slightly. Add the remaining filling ingredients.

3 Preheat the oven to 200°C/400°F/ Gas 6. Put a baking tray in the oven to preheat. Cut one-third off the pastry for the lid. Roll out the remaining pastry and line a 23cm/9in loose-based flan tin. Press the pastry into the edges and make a lip around the top edge. Remove any excess pastry. Pour the filling into the flan case.

4 Roll out the remaining pastry and cut it with a lattice pastry cutter. Carefully open the lattice. Using a rolling pin, lay it over the flan. Brush the joins with egg glaze. Press the edges together and trim off any excess. Brush the lattice with egg glaze and bake for 40 minutes, until golden brown. Serve hot or cold.

CHESTNUT AND MUSHROOM LOAF

You can prepare this dish ahead, freezing it unbaked. Thaw at room temperature overnight before baking.

INGREDIENTS

*45ml/3 tbsp olive oil, plus extra for
brushing
2 medium onions, chopped
2 cloves garlic, chopped
75g/3oz/1¼ cups chopped button
mushrooms
100ml/4fl oz/½ cup red wine
225g/8oz can unsweetened chestnut purée
50g/2oz/1 cup fresh wholemeal
breadcrumbs
salt and freshly ground black pepper
75g/3oz/¾ cup fresh cranberries, plus
extra to decorate
450g/1lb pastry
flour for dusting
1 small egg, beaten, to glaze*

Serves 8

1 Preheat the oven to 190°C/375°F/
Gas 5. Heat the oil in a pan and fry the
onions over a medium heat until they
are translucent. This will take about
7–8 minutes. Add the chopped garlic
and mushrooms and fry for a further
3 minutes. Pour in the wine, stir well
and simmer over a low heat until it
has evaporated, stirring occasionally.
Remove from the heat, stir in the
chestnut purée and breadcrumbs and
season with salt and pepper. Set aside

2 Simmer the cranberries in a little
water for 5 minutes until they start to
pop then drain and leave to cool.

3 Lightly brush a 600ml/1 pint/2½ cup
loaf tin with oil. On a lightly floured
surface, roll out the pastry to a
thickness of about 3mm/⅛in. Cut
rectangles to fit the base and sides of
the tin and press them in place. Press
the edges together to seal them. Cut
a piece of pastry to fit the top of the
tin and set it aside.

4 Spoon half the chestnut mixture
into the tin and level the surface.
Sprinkle on a layer of the cranberries
and cover with the remaining chestnut
mixture. Cover the filling with the pastry
lid and pinch the edges to join them to
the sides. Dust the work surface with
flour, then cut shapes from the pastry
trimmings to use as decorations.

5 Brush the pastry top and the
decorative shapes with the beaten
egg glaze and arrange the shapes in
a pattern on top.

6 Bake the loaf in the oven for
35 minutes, or until the top is golden
brown. Decorate the top with fresh
cranberries. Serve hot.

Spiced Vegetable Couscous

Couscous, a cereal processed from semolina, is used throughout North Africa, mostly in Morocco.

It is traditionally served with Moroccan vegetable stews or tagines but makes a fabulous alternative

Christmas dish. You can serve it on its own or with roasted meat or poultry.

INGREDIENTS

45ml/3 tbsp vegetable oil
1 large onion, finely chopped
2 garlic cloves, crushed
15ml/1 tbsp tomato purée
2.5ml/½ tsp ground turmeric
2.5ml/½ tsp cayenne pepper
5ml/1 tsp ground coriander
5ml/1 tsp ground cumin
225g/8oz/1½ cups cauliflower florets
225g/8oz baby carrots
1 red pepper, seeded and diced
4 beefsteak tomatoes
225g/8oz/1¼ cups thickly sliced courgettes
400g/14oz can chick-peas, drained and rinsed
45ml/3 tbsp chopped fresh coriander
salt and freshly ground black pepper
coriander sprigs, to garnish

For the Couscous
450g/1lb/2⅔ cups couscous
5ml/1 tsp salt
50g/2oz/2 tbsp butter

Serves 6

1 Heat 30ml/2 tbsp of the oil in a large pan, add the onion and garlic, and cook until soft and translucent. Stir in the tomato purée, turmeric, cayenne, ground coriander and cumin. Cook, stirring, for 2 minutes.

2 Add the cauliflower, carrots and pepper, with enough water to come halfway up the vegetables. Bring to the boil, then lower the heat, cover and simmer for 10 minutes.

3 Plunge the tomatoes into boiling water for 30 seconds, then refresh in cold water. Peel away the skins and chop. Add the sliced courgettes, chick-peas and tomatoes to the other vegetables and cook for a further 10 minutes. Stir in the fresh coriander and season with salt and pepper. Set aside and keep hot.

4 To cook the couscous, bring 475ml/16fl oz/2 cups water to the boil in a large saucepan. Add the remaining oil and the salt. Remove from the heat, and add the couscous, stirring. Allow to swell for 2 minutes, then add the butter, and heat through gently, stirring to separate the grains.

5 Turn the couscous out on to a warm serving dish, and spoon the vegetables on top, pouring over any liquid. Garnish with the coriander sprigs and serve at once.

COOK'S TIP

Beefsteak tomatoes have excellent flavour and are ideal for this recipe, but you can substitute six ordinary tomatoes or two 400g/14oz cans chopped tomatoes, if beefsteak tomatoes are not available.

Filo Vegetable Pie

This stunning pie packed with winter vegetables and other goodies makes a delicious main course

for vegetarians. For meat-eaters, it is an excellent accompaniment to

cold sliced turkey or other meat dishes.

INGREDIENTS

225g/8oz leeks
165g/5½oz/11 tbsp butter
225g/8oz carrots, cubed
225g/8oz/3 cups sliced mushrooms
225g/8oz Brussels sprouts, quartered
2 garlic cloves, crushed
115g/4oz/½ cup cream cheese
115g/4oz/½ cup Roquefort or Stilton cheese
150ml/¼ pint/⅔ cup double cream
2 eggs, beaten
225g/8oz cooking apples
225g/8oz/1 cup cashew nuts or pine nuts, toasted
350g/12oz frozen filo pastry, defrosted
salt and freshly ground black pepper

Serves 6–8

3 Whisk the cream cheese and blue cheese, cream, eggs and seasoning together in a bowl. Pour them over the vegetables. Peel and core the apples and cut into 1cm/½in cubes. Stir them into the vegetables. Lastly, add the toasted cashew or pine nuts.

5 Spoon in the vegetable mixture and fold over the excess filo pastry to cover the filling.

6 Brush the remaining filo sheets with butter and cut them into 2.5cm/1in strips. Cover the top of the pie with these strips, arranging them in a rough mound. Bake for 35–45 minutes until golden brown all over. Allow to stand for 5 minutes, and then unclip the spring and gently remove the cake tin. Transfer the pie to a large serving plate.

1 Preheat the oven to 180°C/350°F/ Gas 4. Cut the leeks in half through the root and wash them, separating the layers slightly to check they are clean. Slice into 1cm/½in pieces, drain and dry.

2 Heat 40g/1½oz/3 tbsp of the butter in a large pan and cook the leeks and carrots covered over a medium heat for 5 minutes. Add the mushrooms, sprouts and garlic and cook for another 2 minutes. Turn the vegetables into a bowl and let them cool.

4 Melt the remaining butter. Brush all over the inside of a 23cm/9in loose-based springform cake tin with melted butter. Brush two-thirds of the filo pastry sheets with butter, one sheet at a time, and use them to line the base and sides of the tin, overlapping the layers so that there are no gaps for the filling to fall through.

COOK'S TIP

When working with filo pastry, always keep the sheets you are not using under a clean, damp cloth to prevent them from drying out.

PUMPKIN GNOCCHI

Gnocchi is an Italian pasta dumpling usually made from potatoes; in this special recipe,

pumpkin is added, too. A chanterelle sauce provides both richness and flavour.

INGREDIENTS

450g/1lb floury potatoes, peeled
450g/1lb peeled pumpkin, chopped
2 egg yolks
200g/7oz/1¾ cups plain flour
pinch of ground allspice
1.5ml/¼ tsp ground cinnamon
pinch of grated nutmeg
finely grated rind of ½ orange
salt and freshly ground black pepper

For the Sauce
30ml/2 tbsp olive oil
1 shallot
175g/6oz chanterelles, sliced, or
15g/½oz/¼ cup dried, soaked for
20 minutes in warm water
10ml/2 tsp almond butter
150ml/¼ pint/⅔ cup crème fraîche
a little milk or water
75ml/5 tbsp chopped fresh parsley
50g/2oz/½ cup grated Parmesan cheese

Serves 4

1 Cover the potatoes with cold salted water, bring to the boil and cook for 20 minutes. Drain and set aside. Wrap the pumpkin in foil and bake at 180°C/350°F/Gas 4 for 30 minutes. Drain well, then add to the potato and pass through a vegetable mill into a bowl. Add the egg yolks, flour, spices, orange rind and seasoning and mix well to make a soft dough. Add more flour if necessary.

2 Bring a large pan of salted water to the boil, then dredge a work surface with plain flour. Spoon the gnocchi mixture into a piping bag fitted with a 1cm/½in plain nozzle. Pipe on to the floured surface to make a 15cm/6in sausage shape. Roll in flour and cut into 2.5cm/1in pieces. Repeat the process, making more sausage shapes, until the dough is used up. Mark each gnocchi lightly with a fork and cook for 3–4 minutes in the boiling water.

3 Meanwhile, make the sauce. Heat the oil in a non-stick frying pan. Add the shallot and fry until soft without colouring. Add the chanterelles and cook briefly, then add the almond butter. Stir to melt, and stir in the crème fraîche. Simmer briefly and adjust the consistency with milk or water. Add the parsley and season to taste.

Right: This Spinach and Ricotta Gnocchi makes a quick variation. Cook 900g/2lb spinach in a saucepan and process in a food processor. Mix with 350g/12oz/ 1½ cups ricotta cheese, 60ml/4 tbsp freshly grated Parmesan and 3 beaten eggs. Season to taste. Add enough plain flour to make a soft dough and shape into 7.5cm/3in sausages. Cook the gnocchi in salted boiling water for 1–2 minutes. Transfer to a dish, pour over 115g/4oz/½ cup melted butter and sprinkle with grated Parmesan, to serve.

4 Lift the gnocchi out of the water with a slotted spoon, turn into warmed bowls and spoon the chanterelle sauce over the top. Scatter with the grated Parmesan cheese and serve at once.

COOK'S TIP

If you are planning ahead, gnocchi can be shaped and ready for cooking up to 8 hours in advance. Almond butter is available ready-made from health food shops.

Festive Brussels Sprouts

Be sure to allow plenty of time to peel the chestnuts; they are very fiddly but well worth the effort.

INGREDIENTS

450g/1lb fresh chestnuts
450ml/¾ pint/1⅞ cups vegetable stock
450g/1lb Brussels sprouts
450g/1lb carrots
25g/1oz/2 tbsp butter
salt and freshly ground black pepper

Serves 8

1 Peel the raw chestnuts, leaving the brown papery skins intact. Bringing a small pan of water to the boil, drop the chestnuts into the water for a few minutes, and remove with a slotted spoon. The skins should slip off easily.

2 Put the peeled chestnuts in a pan with the stock. Cover and bring to the boil. Simmer for 10 minutes. Drain.

3 Peel and trim the sprouts. Boil in salted water for 5 minutes. Drain.

4 Cut the carrots in 1cm/½in diagonal slices. Put them in a pan with cold water to cover, bring to the boil and simmer for 6 minutes. Drain. Melt the butter in a clean pan, add the chestnuts, sprouts and carrots and season. Serve hot.

CREAMY SPINACH PURÉE

Crème fraîche, the thick French soured cream, or béchamel sauce usually gives this spinach recipe

its creamy richness, but try this quick, light alternative.

INGREDIENTS

675g/1½lb leaf spinach, stems removed
115g/4oz/1 cup full- or medium-fat soft
cheese
milk (if needed)
freshly grated nutmeg
salt and freshly ground black pepper

Serves 4

1 Rinse the spinach thoroughly under running water. Shake lightly and place in a deep frying pan or wok with just the water clinging to the leaves. Cook, uncovered, over a medium heat for 3–4 minutes until wilted. Drain the spinach in a colander or large sieve, pressing out the excess moisture with the back of a spoon; the spinach doesn't need to be completely dry.

3 Season the spinach with salt, pepper and nutmeg. Transfer to a heavy pan and reheat gently over a low heat. Place in a serving dish and serve hot.

COOK'S TIP

You could also make this purée using Brussels sprouts, if preferred.

2 In a food processor fitted with a metal blade, purée the spinach and soft cheese until well blended, then transfer the mixture to a large bowl. If the purée is too thick to fall easily from a spoon, add a little of the milk, spoonful by spoonful.

Leek and Onion Tart

This unusual recipe isn't a normal tart with pastry, but an all-in-one savoury slice

that is excellent served as an accompaniment to roast meat.

INGREDIENTS

50g/2oz/4 tbsp unsalted butter
350g/12oz leeks, sliced thinly
350g/12oz onions, sliced thinly
225g/8oz/2 cups self-raising flour
115g/4oz/½ cup hard white fat
150ml/¼ pint/⅔ cup water
salt and freshly ground black pepper

Serves 4

1 Preheat the oven to 200°C/400°F/ Gas 6. Melt the butter in a pan and sauté the leeks and onions until soft. Season well with salt and black pepper.

2 Mix the flour, fat and water together in a large bowl to make a soft but sticky dough. Mix into the leek mixture in the pan. Place the contents of the pan in a greased shallow ovenproof dish and level the surface with a palette knife. Bake in the preheated oven for about 30 minutes, or until brown and crispy. Serve the tart sliced, as a vegetable side dish.

COOK'S TIP

Onions keep very well stored in a cool, dry place. Do not store them in the fridge as they will go soft, and never keep cut onions in the fridge unless you want onion-scented milk and an onion-scented home.

THYME-ROASTED ONIONS

These slow-roasted onions develop a delicious, sweet flavour which is the perfect accompaniment

to roast meat. You could prepare par-boiled new potatoes in the same way.

INGREDIENTS

75ml/5 tbsp olive oil
50g/2oz/4 tbsp unsalted butter
900g/2lb small onions
30ml/2 tbsp chopped fresh thyme
salt and freshly ground black pepper

Serves 4

COOK'S TIP

Baby yellow or vidalia onions would be perfect for use in this dish as both types are recommended for slow-roasting. Shallots could be used as a very pleasant alternative as they taste excellent cooked in this way.

2 Add the thyme and seasoning and roast for 45 minutes, basting regularly.

1 Preheat the oven to 220°C/425°F/ Gas 7. Heat the oil and butter in a large roasting tin. Remove the outer skin layer from the onions but keep them whole. Add the onions to the roasting tin and toss them in the oil and butter mixture over a medium heat until they are very lightly sautéed.

Sweet and Sour Red Cabbage

This cabbage dish can be cooked the day before and reheated for serving. It is a good

accompaniment to goose, pork or strong-flavoured game dishes.

INGREDIENTS

900g/2lb red cabbage
30ml/2 tbsp olive oil
2 large onions, sliced
2 large cooking apples, peeled, cored and sliced
30ml/2 tbsp cider vinegar
30ml/2 tbsp soft light brown sugar
225g/8oz rindless streaky bacon, chopped (optional)
salt and freshly ground black pepper

Serves 8

1 Preheat the oven to 180°C/350°F/ Gas 4. Cut the cabbage into quarters and shred it finely with a sharp knife.

2 Heat the oil in a large ovenproof casserole. Cook the onion over a gentle heat for 2 minutes.

3 Stir the cabbage, apples, vinegar, sugar and seasoning into the casserole. Cover and cook for 1 hour, until tender. Stir halfway through cooking.

4 Fry the bacon, if using, until crisp. Stir it into the cabbage before serving.

PARSNIP AND CHESTNUT CROQUETTES

This is a delightful way to present classic Christmas vegetables.

INGREDIENTS

*450g/1lb parsnips, cut roughly into small
pieces
115g/4oz frozen chestnuts
25g/1oz/2 tbsp butter
1 garlic clove, crushed
15ml/1 tbsp chopped fresh coriander
1 egg, beaten
40–50g/1½–2 oz/½ cup fresh white
breadcrumbs
vegetable oil, for frying
salt and freshly ground black pepper
sprig of coriander, to garnish*

Makes 10–12

1 Place the parsnips in a saucepan
with enough water to cover. Bring to the
boil, cover and simmer for about
15–20 minutes, until completely tender.

2 Place the frozen chestnuts in a pan of
water, bring to the boil and simmer for
8–10 minutes, until very tender. Drain,
then place the chestnuts in
a mixing bowl and mash roughly.

3 Melt the butter in a small saucepan
and cook the garlic for 30 seconds.
Drain the parsnips and mash with the
garlic butter. Stir in the chestnuts and
chopped coriander, then season well.

4 Take about 15ml/1 tbsp of the
mixture at a time and form into croquettes, 7.5cm/3in long. Dip into the
beaten egg, then roll in breadcrumbs.

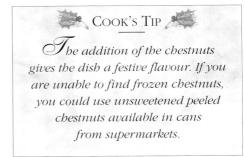

5 Heat a little oil in a frying pan and fry
the croquettes for 3–4 minutes until
golden, turning frequently so they
brown evenly. Drain on kitchen paper
and then serve at once, garnished with
the fresh coriander sprig.

COOK'S TIP

*The addition of the chestnuts
gives the dish a festive flavour. If you
are unable to find frozen chestnuts,
you could use unsweetened peeled
chestnuts available in cans
from supermarkets.*

GLAZED CARROTS WITH CIDER

This recipe is extremely simple to make. The carrots are cooked in the minimum of liquid

to bring out the best of their flavour, and the cider adds a pleasant sharpness.

INGREDIENTS

450g/1lb young carrots
25g/1oz/2 tbsp butter
15ml/1 tbsp soft light brown sugar
120ml/4fl oz/½ cup cider
60ml/4 tbsp vegetable stock or water
5ml/1 tsp Dijon mustard
15ml/1 tbsp finely chopped fresh parsley

Serves 4

1 Trim the tops and bottoms off all of the carrots. Peel or scrape them. Using a sharp knife, cut them into julienne strips.

2 Melt the butter in a heavy-based frying pan, add the carrots and sauté for 4–5 minutes, stirring frequently. Sprinkle with the sugar and cook, stirring for 1 minute or until the sugar has dissolved.

3 Add the cider and stock or water to the frying pan. Bring to the boil and stir in the Dijon mustard. Partially cover the pan with the lid and simmer for about 10–12 minutes, until the carrots are just tender. Remove the lid and continue cooking until the liquid has reduced to a thick sauce.

4 Remove the sauce from the heat and stir in the chopped fresh parsley. Spoon the carrots into a warmed serving dish. Serve as an accompaniment to grilled meat or fish or with a vegetarian dish.

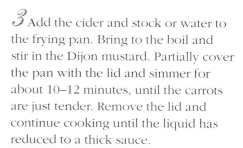

COOK'S TIP

If the carrots are cooked before the liquid in the saucepan has reduced, transfer the carrots to a serving dish and rapidly boil the liquid until thick. Pour over the carrots and sprinkle with parsley.

STIR-FRIED BRUSSELS SPROUTS

Many people are very wary of eating Brussels sprouts because they have had too many

overcooked sprouts served to them in the past. This recipe makes the most of the

vegetable's flavour and has the added interest of an oriental twist.

INGREDIENTS

450g/1lb Brussels sprouts
15ml/1 tbsp sunflower oil
6–8 spring onions, cut into 2.5cm/1in
lengths
2 slices fresh root ginger
40g/1½oz/⅓ cup slivered almonds
150–175ml/4–6fl oz/½–¾ cup vegetable or
chicken stock
salt

Serves 4

1 Remove any large outer leaves and trim the bases of the Brussels sprouts. Cut into slices about 7mm/½in thick.

2 Heat the oil in a wok or heavy-based frying pan, and fry the spring onions and the fresh root ginger for 2–3 minutes, stirring frequently. Add the almonds and stir-fry over a moderate heat until both the onions and almonds begin to brown.

3 Remove and discard the ginger, reduce the heat and stir in the Brussels sprouts. Stir-fry for a few minutes and then pour in the vegetable or chicken stock and cook over a gentle heat for 5–6 minutes, or until the sprouts are nearly tender.

4 Add a little salt to the wok or frying pan, if necessary, and then increase the heat to boil off the excess liquid. Spoon the Brussels sprouts into a warmed serving dish and serve immediately.

COOK'S TIP

If you want to further enhance the oriental flavour of this dish, you could add a couple of dashes of light soy sauce.

PEAS WITH BABY ONIONS AND CREAM

Ideally, use fresh peas and fresh baby onions for this dish. Frozen peas

can be used if fresh ones aren't available, but frozen onions tend to be insipid

and are not worth using. Alternatively, you could use the white part of spring onions.

INGREDIENTS

175g/6oz baby onions
15g/½oz/1 tbsp butter
900g/2lb fresh peas or 350g/12oz/
3 cups shelled or frozen peas
150ml/¼ pint/⅔ cup double cream
15g/½oz/1 tbsp plain flour
10ml/2 tsp chopped fresh parsley
15–30ml/1–2 tbsp lemon juice (optional)
salt and freshly ground black pepper

Serves 4

1 Remove the outer layer of skin from the onions and then halve them, if necessary. Melt the butter in a flameproof casserole and fry the onions for 5–6 minutes over a medium heat, until they just begining to brown and are tender.

2 Add the peas and stir-fry for a few minutes. Add 120ml/4fl oz/½ cup water and bring to the boil. Simmer for about 10 minutes until both are tender. There should be a thin layer of water on the base of the pan.

3 Blend the cream with the flour. Remove the frying pan from the heat and stir in the cream, flour and fresh parsley and season to taste.

4 Cook over a gentle heat for about 3–4 minutes, until the sauce is thick. Add a little lemon juice, if using.

FRENCH BEANS WITH BACON AND CREAM

This baked vegetable accompaniment is rich and full of flavour. It would taste particularly

good served alongside any number of chicken dishes.

INGREDIENTS

350g/12oz French beans
50–75g/2–3oz bacon, chopped
25g/1oz/2 tbsp butter or margarine
15ml/1 tbsp plain flour
350ml/12fl oz/1½ cups milk and single cream, mixed
salt and freshly ground black pepper

Serves 4

1 Preheat the oven to 190°C/375°F/ Gas 5. Trim the beans and cook in lightly salted boiling water for about 5 minutes until just tender. Drain and place them in an ovenproof dish.

2 Dry fry the bacon until crisp, stirring it constantly to make sure that it doesn't stick to the frying pan. Crumble the bacon into very small pieces. Stir into the ovenproof dish with the beans and set aside.

3 Melt the butter or margarine in a large saucepan, stir in the flour and then add the milk and cream to make a smooth sauce, stirring continuously. Season well with plenty of salt and freshly ground black pepper.

4 Pour the sauce over the beans and bacon in the dish and carefully mix it in. Cover the dish lightly with a piece of foil and bake in the preheated oven for 15–20 minutes until hot. Serve immediately.

GRATIN DAUPHINOIS

This dish can be made and baked in advance; reheat it in the oven for 20–30 minutes before serving.

This is a good alternative to roast potatoes and needs no last-minute attention.

INGREDIENTS

butter, for greasing
1.75kg/4lb potatoes
2–3 garlic cloves, crushed
2.5ml/½ tsp grated nutmeg
115g/4oz/1 cup grated Cheddar cheese
600ml/1 pint/2½ cups milk
300ml/½ pint/1¼ cups single cream
2 large eggs, beaten
salt and freshly ground black pepper

Serves 8

COOK'S TIP

The best type of potatoes to use in this dish are Golden Wonder or Kerr's Pink. For the cheese, use a full-flavoured farmhouse Cheddar for the most satisfying taste.

1 Preheat the oven to 180°C/350°F/ Gas 4. Butter a 2.4 litre/4 pint/10 cup shallow ovenproof dish. Peel the potatoes, using a potato peeler or a sharp knife, and slice them thinly. If you have a food processor, slice the potatoes in it, using the metal blade.

2 Layer the potato slices in the dish. Add the crushed garlic, nutmeg and two-thirds of the grated Cheddar cheese in alternate layers with the potato. Season well with salt and freshly ground black pepper.

3 Whisk the milk, cream and eggs together and pour them over the potatoes, making sure the liquid goes all the way to the bottom of the dish.

4 Scatter the remaining cheese on top and bake in the preheated oven for 45–50 minutes or until the top layer is golden brown and the cheese is bubbling. Test the potatoes with a sharp knife; they should be very tender. Serve immediately.

Sautéed Potatoes

These rosemary-scented, crisp golden potatoes are an extra-special treat at Christmas time.

INGREDIENTS

1.5kg/3lb baking potatoes
60–90ml/4–6 tbsp oil, bacon dripping or
clarified butter
2 or 3 fresh rosemary sprigs, leaves
removed and chopped
salt and freshly ground black pepper

Serves 6

1 Peel the potatoes and cut into 2.5cm/ 1in pieces. Place them in a bowl, cover with cold water and leave to soak for 10–15 minutes. Drain, rinse and drain again, then dry thoroughly in a clean tea towel.

2 In a large, heavy non-stick frying pan or wok, heat about 60ml/4 tbsp of the oil, dripping or butter over a medium-high heat, until very hot, but not smoking.

> ### COOK'S TIP
> *Soaking the potatoes before cooking removes excess starch, resulting in a crispier coating to the cooked potatoes.*

3 Add the potatoes to the frying pan and cook for 2 minutes, without stirring, so that they seal completely and brown on one side.

4 Shake the pan and toss the potatoes to brown them on the other side, and continue to stir and shake the pan until the potatoes are evenly browned all over. Season with salt and pepper.

5 Add a little more oil, dripping or butter to the frying pan and continue cooking the potatoes over a medium-low to low heat for 20–25 minutes, until tender when pierced with a knife. Stir and shake the pan frequently. About 5 minutes before the end of cooking, sprinkle the potatoes with the chopped fresh rosemary sprigs.

Hasselback Potatoes

This is an unusual way to cook with potatoes: each potato half is sliced almost to the base and then

roasted with oil and butter. The crispy potatoes are then coated in an orange glaze and

returned to the oven until deep golden brown and crunchy.

INGREDIENTS

4 large potatoes
25g/1oz/2 tbsp butter, melted
45ml/3 tbsp olive oil

For the Glaze
juice of 1 orange
grated rind of ½ orange
15ml/1 tbsp demerara sugar
freshly ground black pepper

Serves 4–6

1 Preheat the oven to 190°C/375°F/ Gas 5. Cut each potato in half length-ways. If you wish to score the potatoes for decoration, place the flat-side down on the chopping board and then cut down as if making very thin slices, but leaving the bottom 1cm/½in intact.

2 Place the potatoes in a large roasting dish. Using a pastry brush, coat the potatoes generously with the melted butter and pour the olive oil over the base and around the potatoes.

3 Bake the potatoes in the preheated oven for 40–50 minutes, just until they begin to turn brown.

4 Meanwhile, place the orange juice, orange rind and sugar in a small saucepan and heat gently, stirring until the sugar has dissolved. Simmer for 3–4 minutes, until the glaze is fairly thick, and then remove from the heat.

5 When the potatoes begin to brown, brush all over with the orange glaze and return to the oven to roast for a further 15 minutes or until the potatoes are a deep golden brown. Tip onto a warmed serving plate and serve.

Buffet Dishes

The feeding doesn't end with Christmas Day but you can serve turkey leftovers for only so long. When the guests come on Boxing Day or perhaps New Year's Eve, a buffet is the perfect solution. Tarts are one of the easiest dishes to serve and you'll have a wonderful choice here with the Wild Mushroom Tart, Mini Leek and Onion Tartlets and the Turkey and Cranberry Pie. Serve any of these alongside Fillet of Beef with Ratatouille or Classic Whole Salmon, accompanied by Smoked Trout Pilaff or Garden Vegetable Terrine. Provide a little fruit with the tangy Carrot, Apple and Orange Coleslaw and a few nuts with the Celery, Avocado and Walnut Salad, and you're sure to receive a second day's worth of compliments.

Game Terrine

Any game can be used to make this country terrine – hare, rabbit, pheasant or pigeon –

so choose the best meat your butcher has to offer.

INGREDIENTS

225g/8oz rindless, unsmoked streaky bacon
225g/8oz lamb's or pig's liver, minced
450g/1lb minced pork
1 small onion, finely chopped
2 garlic cloves, crushed
10ml/2 tsp mixed dried herbs
225g/8oz game of your choice
60ml/4 tbsp port or sherry
1 bay leaf
50g/2oz/4 tbsp plain flour
300ml/½ pint/1¼ cups aspic jelly, made up as packet instructions
salt and freshly ground black pepper

Serves 8

2 Mix the minced meats with the chopped onion, garlic and mixed dried herbs. Season well with plenty of salt and ground black pepper.

5 Preheat the oven to 160°C/325°F/ Gas 3. Put the flour into a small bowl and mix it to a firm dough with 30–45ml/2–3 tbsp cold water. Cover the terrine with a lid and seal it with the flour paste. Place the terrine in a roasting tin and pour around enough hot water to come halfway up the sides of the tin. Cook in the preheated oven for about 2 hours.

1 Remove the rind from the bacon and stretch each rasher with the back of a heavy kitchen knife. Use the bacon to line a 1 litre/1¾ pint/4 cup terrine. The terrine should be ovenproof and must have a lid to seal in all the flavours during the long cooking time.

3 Use a heavy kitchen knife to cut the game into thin strips, and put the meat into a large mixing bowl with the port or sherry. Season with salt and freshly ground black pepper.

4 Put one-third of the minced mixture into the terrine. Press the mixture well into the corners. Cover with half the strips of the game and repeat these layers, ending with a minced layer. Level the surface and lay the bay leaf on top.

6 Remove the lid and weight the terrine down with a 2kg/4lb weight. Leave to cool. Remove any fat from the surface and cover with warmed aspic jelly. Leave overnight before turning out onto a serving plate. Serve the terrine cut into thin slices with a mixed salad and some fruit-based chutney.

Turkey and Cranberry Pie

The cranberries add a tart layer to this turkey pie. Cranberry sauce can be used

if fresh cranberries are not available. The pie freezes well and is an ideal dish to prepare in advance.

INGREDIENTS

450g/1lb pork sausagemeat
450g/1lb lean minced pork
15ml/1 tbsp ground coriander
15ml/1 tbsp mixed dried herbs
finely grated rind of 2 large oranges
10ml/2 tsp grated fresh root ginger or
2.5ml/½ tsp ground ginger
450g/1 lb turkey breast fillets, thinly sliced
115g/4oz/1 cup fresh cranberries
salt and freshly ground black pepper

For the Pastry
450g/1lb/4 cups plain flour
5ml/1 tsp salt
150g/5oz/⅔ cup lard
150ml/¼ pint/⅔ cup mixed milk and water

To Finish
1 egg, beaten
300ml/½ pint/1¼ cups aspic jelly, made up
as packet instructions

Serves 8

1 Preheat the oven to 180°C/350°F/ Gas 4. Place a large baking tray in the oven to preheat. In a large bowl, mix together the sausagemeat, minced pork, coriander, mixed dried herbs, orange rind and ginger with plenty of salt and freshly ground black pepper.

2 To make the pastry, put the flour into a large bowl with the salt. Heat the lard in a small pan with the milk and water until just beginning to boil. Draw the pan aside and allow to cool slightly.

3 Using a wooden spoon, quickly stir the liquid into the flour until a very stiff dough is formed. Turn on to a work surface and knead until smooth. Cut one-third off the dough for the lid, wrap it in clear film and keep it in a warm place.

4 Roll out the large piece of dough on a floured surface and line the base and sides of a well-greased 20cm/8in loose-based, springform cake tin. Work with the dough while it is still warm, as it will start to crack and break if it is left to get cold.

5 Put the turkey breast fillets between two pieces of clear film and flatten with a rolling pin to a 3mm/⅛in thickness. Spoon half the pork mixture into the base of the tin, pressing it well into the edges. Cover with half of the turkey slices and then the cranberries, followed by the remaining turkey and finally the rest of the pork mixture.

6 Roll out the rest of the dough and cover the filling, trimming any excess and sealing the edges with beaten egg. Make a steam hole in the lid and decorate with pastry trimmings. Brush with beaten egg. Bake for 2 hours. Cover the pie with foil if it gets too brown. Place the pie on a wire rack to cool. When cold, use a funnel to fill the pie with aspic jelly. Allow to set overnight before unmoulding the pie.

FILLET OF BEEF WITH RATATOUILLE

This succulent rare beef is served cold with a colourful garlicky ratatouille.

INGREDIENTS

700–900g/1½–2lb fillet of beef
45ml/3 tbsp olive oil
300ml/½ pint/1¼ cups aspic jelly, made up
as packet instructions

For the Marinade
30ml/2 tbsp sherry
30ml/2 tbsp olive oil
30ml/2 tbsp soy sauce
10ml/2 tsp grated fresh root ginger or
5ml/1 tsp ground ginger
2 garlic cloves, crushed

For the Ratatouille
60ml/4 tbsp olive oil
1 onion, sliced
2–3 garlic cloves, crushed
1 large aubergine, cubed
1 small red pepper, seeded and sliced
1 small green pepper, seeded and sliced
1 small yellow pepper, seeded and sliced
225g/8oz courgettes, sliced
450g/1lb tomatoes, skinned and quartered
15ml/1 tbsp chopped mixed fresh herbs
30ml/2 tbsp French dressing
salt and freshly ground black pepper

Serves 8

1 Mix all the marinade ingredients together in a shallow dish, put the beef in and turn it over to coat it. Cover the dish with clear film and leave for 30 minutes, to allow the flavours to penetrate.

2 Preheat the oven to 220°C/425°F/ Gas 7. Using a large slotted spoon, lift the fillet out of the marinade and pat it dry with kitchen paper. Heat the oil in a frying pan until smoking hot and then brown the beef all over to seal it. Transfer to a roasting tin and roast for 10–15 minutes, basting it occasionally with the marinade. Lift the beef on to a large plate and leave it to cool.

3 Meanwhile, for the ratatouille, heat the oil in a large casserole and cook the onion and garlic over a low heat, until tender, without letting the onions become brown. Add the aubergine cubes to the casserole and cook for a further 5 minutes, until soft. Add the sliced peppers and courgettes and cook for 2 minutes more. Then add the tomatoes, chopped herbs and season well with salt and pepper. Cook for a few minutes longer.

4 Turn the ratatouille into a dish and set aside to cool. Drizzle the ratatouille with a little French dressing. Slice the beef and arrange overlapping slices on a serving platter. Brush the slices with cold aspic jelly that is on the point of setting.

5 Leave the jelly to set completely, then brush with a second coat. Spoon the ratatouille around the beef slices on the platter and serve immediately.

COOK'S TIP

Ratatouille is a traditional French recipe that is at its best when made with the choicest fresh ingredients. It makes a wonderful side dish for a buffet or can be eaten as a snack, as a vegetarian filling for jacket potatoes.

Wild Mushroom Tart

The flavour of wild mushrooms makes this tart really rich: use as wide a variety of

mushrooms as you can get hold of, for added flavour.

INGREDIENTS

For the Pastry
225g/8oz/2 cups plain flour
2.5ml/½ tsp salt
50g/2oz/4 tbsp hard white
vegetable fat
10ml/2 tsp lemon juice
about 150ml/¼ pint/⅔ cup
ice-cold water
115g/4oz/½ cup butter, chilled, cubed
1 egg, beaten

For the Filling
150g/5oz/10 tbsp butter
2 shallots, finely chopped
2 garlic cloves, crushed
450g/1lb mixed wild mushrooms, sliced
45ml/3 tbsp chopped fresh parsley
30ml/2 tbsp double cream
salt and freshly ground black pepper

Serves 6

1 To make the pastry, sieve the flour and salt together into a large mixing bowl. Add the white fat and rub into the mixture until it resembles fine breadcrumbs.

2 Add the lemon juice and enough iced water to make a soft but not too sticky dough. Cover and set aside to chill for 20 minutes.

3 Roll the pastry out into a rectangle on a lightly floured surface. Mark the dough into three equal strips and arrange half the butter cubes over two-thirds of the dough.

4 Fold the outer two-thirds over, folding over the uncovered third last. Seal the edges with a rolling pin. Give the dough a quarter turn and roll it out again. Mark it into thirds and dot with the remaining butter in the same way.

5 Chill the pastry for 20 minutes. Repeat the process of marking into thirds, folding over, giving a quarter turn and rolling out three times, chilling for 20 minutes in between each time. To make the filling, melt 50g/2oz/ 4 tbsp butter and fry the shallots and garlic until soft, but not browned. Add the remaining butter and the mushrooms and cook for 35–40 minutes. Drain off any excess liquid and stir in the remaining ingredients. Leave to cool. Preheat the oven to 220°C/425°F/Gas 7.

6 Divide the pastry in two. Roll out one half into a 23cm/9in round, cutting around a plate to make a neat shape. Pile the filling into the centre. Roll out the remaining pastry large enough to cover the base. Brush the edges of the base with water and then lay the second pastry circle on top. Press the edges together to seal and brush the top with a little beaten egg to glaze. Bake for 45 minutes, or until the pastry is risen, golden and flaky.

Garden Vegetable Terrine

Perfect for a Christmas buffet menu, this is a softly set, creamy terrine of colourful vegetables

wrapped in glossy spinach leaves. Select large spinach leaves for the best results.

INGREDIENTS

225g/8oz fresh leaf spinach
3 carrots, cut in sticks
3–4 long, thin leeks
about 115g/4oz long green beans, topped and tailed
1 red pepper, cut in strips
2 courgettes, cut in sticks
115g/4oz broccoli florets

For the Sauce
1 egg and 2 yolks
300ml/½ pint/1¼ cups single cream
fresh nutmeg, grated
5ml/1 tsp salt
50g/2oz/½ cup grated Cheddar cheese
oil, for greasing
freshly ground black pepper

Serves 6

1 Preheat oven to 180°C/350°F/Gas 4. Blanch the spinach quickly in boiling water, then drain, refresh in cold water and carefully pat dry.

2 Grease a 1kg/2lb loaf tin and line the base with a sheet of greaseproof paper. Line with the spinach leaves, allowing them to overhang the tin.

3 Blanch the rest of the vegetables in boiling, salted water until just tender. Drain and refresh in cold water then, when cool, pat dry with pieces of kitchen paper.

4 Place the vegetables into the loaf tin in a colourful mixture, making sure the sticks of vegetables lie lengthways.

5 Beat the sauce ingredients together and slowly pour over the vegetables. Tap the loaf tin to ensure the sauce seeps into the gaps. Fold over the spinach leaves at the top of the terrine to make a neat surface.

6 Cover the terrine with a sheet of greased foil, then bake in a roasting tin half full of boiling water for about 1–1¼ hours until set.

7 Cool the terrine in the tin, then chill. To serve, loosen the sides and shake out gently. Serve cut in thick slices.

CHICKEN ROLL

This roll can be prepared and cooked the day before it is needed and will freeze well, too.

Remove from the refrigerator about an hour before serving.

INGREDIENTS

2 kg/4lb chicken

For the Stuffing
1 medium onion, finely chopped
50g/2oz/4 tbsp melted butter
350g/12oz lean minced pork
115g/4oz streaky bacon, chopped
15ml/1 tbsp chopped fresh parsley
10ml/2 tsp chopped fresh thyme
115g/4oz/2 cups fresh white breadcrumbs
30ml/2 tbsp sherry
1 large egg, beaten
25g/1oz/¼ cup shelled pistachio nuts
25g/1oz/¼ cup stoned black olives
(about 12)
salt and freshly ground black pepper

Serves 8

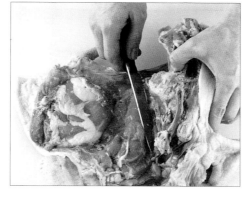

3 Cut the flesh away from the carcass, scraping the bones clean. Carefully cut through the sinew around the leg and wing joints and scrape down the bones to free them. Remove the carcass, taking care not to cut through the skin along the breastbone so that the stuffing will not escape during cooking.

4 To stuff the chicken, lay it flat, skin side down, and level the flesh as much as possible. Shape the stuffing down the centre and fold the sides over.

5 Sew the flesh together, using dark thread (this will be easier to see when the roll is cooked). Tie the flesh with string to form a roll.

6 Preheat the oven to 180°C/350°F/ Gas 4. Place the roll, with the join underneath, on a roasting rack in a roasting tin and brush with the remaining butter. Bake uncovered for about 1¼ hours or until cooked. Baste the chicken often. Leave to cool completely before removing the string and thread. Wrap in foil and chill until ready for serving or freezing.

1 To make the stuffing, cook the chopped onion gently in a frying pan with 25g/1oz/2 tbsp butter until soft. Turn into a bowl and allow to cool. Add the remaining ingredients, mix thoroughly and season well with salt and freshly ground black pepper.

2 Set the chicken on a clean chopping board and bone it. To start, use a small, sharp knife to remove the wing tips Turn the chicken over on to its breast and cut a deep line down the backbone.

Mini Leek and Onion Tartlets

The savoury filling in these tartlets is traditional to France where many types of quiche are popular.

Baking in individual tins makes for easier serving and looks attractive on the buffet table.

INGREDIENTS

25g/1oz/2 tbsp butter, cut into 8 pieces
1 onion, thinly sliced
2.5ml/½ tsp dried thyme
450g/1lb leeks, thinly sliced
50g/2oz/5 tbsp grated Gruyère or Emmenthal cheese
3 eggs
300ml/½ pint/1¼ cups single cream
pinch of freshly grated nutmeg
salt and freshly ground black pepper
lettuce leaves, parsley leaves and cherry tomatoes, to serve

For the Pastry
175g/6oz/1½ cup plain flour
85g/3oz/6 tbsp cold butter
1 egg yolk
30–45ml/2–3 tbsp cold water
2.5ml/½ tsp salt

Serves 6

1 To make the pastry, sift the flour into a bowl and add the butter. Using your fingertips or a pastry blender, rub or cut the butter into the flour until the mixture resembles fine breadcrumbs.

2 Make a well in the flour mixture. In a small bowl, beat together the egg yolk, water and salt. Pour into the well and, using a fork, lightly combine the flour and liquid until the dough begins to stick together. Form into a flattened ball. Wrap and chill for 30 minutes.

3 Lightly butter six 10cm/4in tartlet tins. On a lightly floured surface, roll out the dough until about 3mm/⅛in thick, then using a 13cm/5in fluted cutter, cut out as many rounds as possible. Gently ease the pastry rounds firmly into the base and sides of each tin. Re-roll the trimmings and use to line the remaining tins. Prick the bases all over with a fork and chill for about 30 minutes.

4 Preheat the oven to 190°C/375°F/ Gas 5. Line the pastry cases with foil and fill each one with baking beans or a heaping handful of dried pulses. Place them on a baking sheet and bake for 6–8 minutes until the pastry edges are golden. Lift out the foil and beans and bake the pastry cases for a further 2 minutes until the bases appear dry. Transfer to a wire rack and leave to cool. Reduce the oven temperature to 180°C/350°F/Gas 4.

5 In a large frying pan, melt the butter over a medium heat, then add the onion and thyme and cook for 3–5 minutes until the onion is just softened, stirring frequently. Add the leeks and cook for 10–12 minutes more until they are soft and tender. Divide the mixture among the cooled pastry cases and sprinkle the top of each tartlet with cheese, dividing it evenly between them.

6 In a medium-size bowl, beat together the eggs, cream, nutmeg and salt and pepper. Place the pastry cases on a baking sheet and slowly pour in the egg mixture, being careful not to let them overflow. Bake for 15–20 minutes until set and golden. Transfer the tartlets to a wire rack to cool slightly, then remove them from the tins and serve warm or at room temperature, with a mixture of lettuce and parsley leaves and cherry tomatoes.

Classic Whole Salmon

Serving a boneless whole salmon is a delight. If you own a fish kettle the method is slightly different:

cover the salmon with water and a dash of white wine, add a bay leaf, sliced lemon and black

peppercorns and bring to the boil for 6 minutes. Leave to cool completely in the water until cold.

Drain, pat dry, and continue as instructed in the recipe.

INGREDIENTS

1 whole salmon
3 bay leaves
1 lemon, sliced
12 black peppercorns
300ml/½ pint/1¼ cups water
150ml/¼ pint/⅔ cup white wine
2 cucumbers, thinly sliced
large bunches of mixed fresh herbs such
as parsley, chervil and chives, to
garnish
mayonnaise, to serve

Serves 8

1 Preheat the oven to 180°C/350°F/ Gas 4. Clean the inside of the salmon. Make sure all the gut has been removed and the inside cavity has been well rinsed in several changes of cold water and then wiped out with kitchen paper. Cut the tail into a neat "V" shape with a sharp pair of kitchen scissors. Place the fish on a large piece of double thickness foil. Lay the bay leaves, sliced lemon and black peppercorns inside the cavity. Wrap the foil around the fish and up the sides, and pour on the water and wine. Seal the parcel tightly and place in a large roasting tin.

2 Bake in the preheated oven, allowing 15 minutes per pound plus 15 minutes extra. Remove from the oven, and, being careful not to scald yourself on the steam, open up the parcel. Leave to cool. Don't be tempted to leave the salmon to chill overnight as the skin will be impossible to remove the next day.

3 Using a sharp knife or a sharp pair of kitchen scissors, cut off the head and tail, reserving them if you want to display the fish later. Turn the fish upside-down on to a board so the flattest side is uppermost. Carefully peel off the base foil and the skin. Using a sharp knife, gently scrape away any excess brown flesh from the pink salmon flesh.

4 Make an incision down the back fillet, drawing the flesh away from the central bone. Take one fillet and place on the serving dish. Remove the second fillet and place it beside the first to form the base of the fish.

5 Then carefully remove the central backbone from the salmon. Place the other half of the fish with the skin still intact, flesh-side down, on top of the base fish. Peel off the upper skin and any brown bits. Replace the head and tail if required. Using the cucumber slices, lay them on top of the fish, working from the tail end until all the flesh is covered and the cucumber resembles scales. Garnish the serving plate with the fresh herbs of your choice. Serve with mayonnaise.

Layered Salmon Terrine

This elegant fish mousse is perfect for a Christmas buffet table or as a starter course.

INGREDIENTS

200ml/7fl oz/⅞ cup milk
50g/2oz/4 tbsp butter
65g/2½oz/⅔ cup plain flour
450g/1lb fresh haddock fillet, boned and skinned
450g/1lb fresh salmon fillet, boned and skinned
2 eggs, beaten
60ml/4 tbsp double cream
115g/4oz smoked salmon or trout, cut in strips
salt and freshly ground black pepper

Serves 8

1 Heat the milk and butter in a saucepan until the milk is boiling. Draw the saucepan aside and beat in the flour until a thick, smooth paste forms. Season well with salt and freshly ground black pepper, and turn the flour paste out on to a plate and leave to cool.

2 Put the haddock into a food processor and process it until smooth. Put it into a bowl. Process the salmon fillet in the same way and put it into a separate bowl. Add an egg and half the cream to each of the fish mixtures. Then beat in half the milk and flour paste to each mixture.

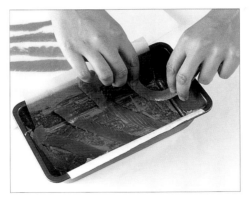

3 Preheat the oven to 180°C/350°F/Gas 4. Butter a 900g/2lb loaf tin and line it with a piece of greaseproof paper. Lay strips of smoked salmon or trout diagonally over the base and up the side of the lined tin.

4 Spoon the haddock mixture into the tin and level the surface. Cover with the salmon mixture and level the surface.

5 Cover the tin with a layer of buttered greaseproof paper and a layer of foil. Place it in a roasting tin and half fill the tin with hot water. Cook for 40 minutes.

6 Remove the terrine from the oven and let stand for 10 minutes. Turn the terrine out of the loaf tin and serve it warm or leave it to cool, as preferred.

Smoked Trout Pilaff

Smoked trout might seem an unusual partner for rice, but this is a winning combination with an original

Indian-influenced flavour that will be well appreciated at Christmas time.

INGREDIENTS

225g/8oz/1¼ cups white basmati rice
40g/1½oz/3 tbsp butter
2 onions, sliced into rings
1 garlic clove, crushed
2 bay leaves
2 whole cloves
2 green cardamom pods
2 cinnamon sticks
5ml/1 tsp cumin seeds
4 smoked trout fillets, skinned
50g/2oz/½ cup slivered almonds, toasted
50g/2oz/⅓ cup seedless raisins
30ml/2 tbsp chopped fresh parsley
mango chutney and poppadums, to serve

Serves 4

COOK'S TIP

The use of the mango chutney and poppadums as a serving suggestion with this dish really rings the changes and shows that alternative fare at Christmas can be no less festive. Ready-made poppadums can easily be found in specialist shops and supermarkets. They can be heated in the oven or a microwave in just a few minutes.

1 Wash the rice thoroughly in several changes of water and drain well. Set aside. Melt the butter in a large frying pan and fry the onions until well browned, stirring frequently.

2 Add the garlic, bay leaves, cloves, cardamom pods, cinnamon sticks and cumin seeds and stir-fry for 1 minute.

3 Stir in the rice, then add 600ml/ 1 pint/2½ cups boiling water. Bring to the boil. Cover the pan tightly, reduce the heat and cook very gently for 20–25 minutes, until the water has been absorbed and the rice is tender.

4 Flake the smoked trout and add to the pan with the almonds and raisins. Fork through gently. Re-cover the pan and allow the smoked trout to warm in the rice for a few minutes. Remove the spices and bay leaves. Scatter over the parsley and serve with mango chutney and poppadums.

Tomato and Basil Tart

This mouthwatering savoury tart will be very popular at buffet parties, and vegetarians will love it, too.

It is a very simple tart to make, with rich shortcrust pastry, topped with slices of mozzarella cheese

and tomatoes and enriched with olive oil and basil leaves.

INGREDIENTS

150g/5oz mozzarella, thinly sliced
4 large tomatoes, thickly sliced
about 10 basil leaves
30ml/2 tbsp olive oil
2 garlic cloves, thinly sliced
sea salt and freshly ground black pepper

For the Pastry
115g/4oz/1 cup plain flour
pinch of salt
50g/2oz/4 tbsp butter or margarine
1 egg yolk

Serves 4

1 To prepare the pastry, mix together the flour and salt, then rub in the butter and egg yolk. Add enough cold water to make a smooth dough and knead lightly on a floured surface. Place in a plastic bag and chill for about 1 hour.

2 Preheat the oven to 190°C/375°F/Gas 5. Remove the pastry from the fridge, and allow about 10 minutes for it to return to room temperature and then roll out into a 20cm/8in round. Press into the base of a 20cm/8in flan dish or tin. Prick the case all over with a fork and then bake in the oven for about 10 minutes until firm but not brown. Allow to cool slightly. Reduce the oven temperature to 180°C/350°F/Gas 4.

3 Arrange the mozzarella slices over the pastry base. On top, arrange a single layer of the sliced tomatoes, overlapping them slightly. Dip the basil leaves in olive oil and arrange them on the tomatoes.

4 Scatter the garlic on top, drizzle with the remaining olive oil and season with a little salt and a good sprinkling of black pepper. Bake for 40–45 minutes, until the tomatoes are well cooked. Serve hot or at room temperature.

COOK'S TIP

Pricking the base or sides of the pastry before it goes into the oven ensures the tart does not puff up during the cooking time, making it easier to fill. If the cheese exudes a lot of liquid during baking, tilt the flan dish and spoon it off to keep the pastry from becoming soggy.

Turkey Rice Salad

A delicious, crunchy salad to use up leftover turkey during the holiday festivities.

Ingredients

225g/8oz/1¼ cups brown rice
50g/2oz/⅔ cup wild rice
2 red dessert apples, quartered, cored and
chopped
2 celery sticks, coarsely sliced
115g/4oz seedless grapes
45ml/3 tbsp lemon or orange juice
150ml/¼ pint/⅔ cup thick mayonnaise
350g/12oz cooked turkey, chopped
salt and freshly ground black pepper
frilly lettuce leaves, to serve

Serves 8

1 Cook the brown and wild rice in boiling salted water for 25 minutes or until tender. Rinse under cold running water and drain.

2 Turn the well-drained rice into a large bowl and add the apples, celery and grapes. Beat the lemon or orange juice into the mayonnaise, season with salt and pepper and pour over the rice.

3 Add the turkey and mix well to coat with the lemon or orange mayonnaise.

4 Arrange the frilly lettuce leaves over the base and around the sides of a warmed serving dish and spoon the rice on top.

Ham and Bulgur Wheat Salad

This flavoursome, nutty salad is ideal for using up leftover cooked ham for a quick and

simple addition to a Christmas buffet menu.

INGREDIENTS

225g/8oz/1⅓ cup bulgur wheat
45ml/3 tbsp olive oil
30ml/2 tbsp lemon juice
1 red pepper
225g/8oz cooked ham, diced
30ml/2 tbsp chopped fresh mint
30ml/2 tbsp currants
salt and freshly ground black pepper
sprigs of fresh mint and lemon slices, to garnish

Serves 8

3 Quarter the pepper, removing the stalk and seeds. Rinse under running water. Using a sharp knife, cut the pepper quarters cut into wide strips and then into diamonds.

4 Add the pepper, ham, chopped fresh mint and currants to the wheat in the bowl. Mix with a spoon to ensure the ingredients are well distributed, then transfer the salad to a serving dish, garnish with the fresh mint sprigs and lemon slices and serve.

> ### COOK'S TIP
>
> *This salad can also be made with 225g/8oz/1⅓ cup couscous instead of the bulgur wheat. To prepare, cover the couscous with boiling water as in Step 1.*

1 Put the bulgur wheat into a bowl, pour over enough boiling water to cover and leave to stand until all the water has been absorbed and the grains look as if they have swelled up.

2 Add the oil, lemon juice, and seasoning to taste. Toss to separate the grains using two forks.

Celery, Avocado and Walnut Salad

The crunchiness of the celery and walnuts contrasts perfectly with the smooth avocado.

Serve it with a soured cream dressing as suggested or simply dressed with a little

extra-virgin olive oil and freshly squeezed lemon juice.

INGREDIENTS

3 bacon rashers (optional)
8 tender white or green celery sticks, very thinly sliced
3 spring onions, finely chopped
50g/2oz/½ cup chopped walnuts
1 ripe avocado
lemon juice

For the Dressing
120ml/4fl oz/½ cup soured cream
15ml/1 tbsp extra-virgin olive oil
pinch of cayenne pepper

Serves 4

1 Dry fry the bacon, if using, until golden and then chop into small pieces and place in a salad bowl with the celery, spring onions and walnuts.

2 Halve the avocado and, using a very sharp knife, cut into thin slices. Peel away the skin from each slice and sprinkle generously with lemon juice and add to the celery mixture.

3 Lightly beat the soured cream, olive oil and cayenne pepper together in a jug or small bowl. Either fold carefully into the salad or serve separately.

COOK'S TIP

Whenever you need to prepare avocado for a salad dish, sprinkle it liberally with lemon juice to prevent the flesh from discolouring before the dish is served.

Carrot, Apple and Orange Coleslaw

This dish is as delicious as it is easy to make. The garlic and herb dressing adds the

necessary contrast to the sweetness of the salad.

INGREDIENTS

350g/12oz young carrots, finely grated
2 eating apples
15ml/1 tbsp lemon juice
1 large orange

For the Dressing
45ml/3 tbsp olive oil
60ml/4 tbsp sunflower oil
45ml/3 tbsp lemon juice
1 garlic clove, crushed
60ml/4 tbsp natural yogurt
15ml/1 tbsp chopped mixed fresh herbs
such as tarragon, parsley or chives
salt and freshly ground black pepper

Serves 4

1 Place the carrots in a large serving bowl. Quarter the apples, remove the core and then slice thinly. Sprinkle them with the lemon juice, to prevent them from discolouring, and then add to the carrots.

2 Using a sharp knife, remove the peel and pith from the orange and then separate it into segments. Add to the carrots and apples.

3 To make the dressing, place both the oils with the lemon juice, crushed garlic, natural yogurt, mixed fresh herbs and seasoning in a jar with a lid and shake to blend.

4 Just before serving, pour the dressing over the salad and toss well together to mix.

> ### COOK'S TIP
> *You can prepare the dressing in advance and keep it in the fridge for up to a week.*

Party Foods

𝒢one are the days of an uninspiring bowl of peanuts or a mediocre choice of cheeses and canapés. The tremendous range of ingredients available in the shops nowadays means that there are endless possibilities for lavish festive party foods. Try mixing a few of these fabulous dishes for a truly international taste: Tapas of Almonds, Olives and Cheese, Prawn Toasts and Hot Salt Beef on a Stick would always go together well. For vegetarians, try Mini Filled Jacket Potatoes and Spicy Sun-dried Tomato Pizza Wedges. Spoil your guests with mincemeat-filled Filo Crackers or provide a Rich Chocolate and Fruit Fondue, and see them welcome in the New Year around the cooking pot.

CHEESELETS

These crispy cheese biscuits are irresistible, and will disappear in moments.

INGREDIENTS

115g/4oz/1 cup plain flour
2.5ml/½ tsp salt
2.5ml/½ tsp cayenne pepper
2.5ml/½ tsp dry mustard
115g/4oz/½ cup butter
50g/2oz/½ cup grated Cheddar cheese
50g/2oz/½ cup grated Gruyère cheese
1 egg white, beaten
15g/1 tbsp sesame seeds

Makes about 80

1 Preheat the oven to 220°C/425°F/ Gas 7. Line several baking sheets with non-stick baking paper. Sift the flour, salt, cayenne pepper and mustard into a mixing bowl. Cut the butter into pieces and rub into the flour mixture.

2 Divide the mixture in half, add the Cheddar to one half and the Gruyère to the other. Using a fork or your fingertips, work each mixture into a soft dough and knead on a floured surface until smooth.

3 Roll out both pieces of dough very thinly and cut into 2.5cm/1in squares. Transfer to the lined baking sheets. Brush the squares with beaten egg white, sprinkle with sesame seeds and bake for 5–6 minutes or until slightly puffed up and pale gold in colour. Cool on the baking sheets, then carefully remove with a palette knife. Repeat the process until you have used up all the biscuit dough. Pack the biscuits in airtight tins or present as a gift, packed in boxes tied with ribbon.

VARIATION

Try using different cheeses sprinkled with a variety of seeds to give alternative flavours.

Cocktail Biscuits

Tiny savoury biscuits are always a welcome treat.

Experiment with different flavours and shapes and make a batch of biscuits to give as gifts.

INGREDIENTS

350g/12oz/3 cups plain flour
2.5ml/½ tsp salt
2.5ml/½ tsp black pepper
5ml/1 tsp wholegrain mustard
175g/6oz/¾ cup butter
115g/4oz/½ cup grated Cheddar
1 egg, beaten

Flavourings
5ml/1 tsp chopped nuts
10ml/2 tsp dill seeds
10ml/2 tsp curry paste
10ml/2 tsp chilli sauce

Makes about 80

1 Preheat the oven to 200°C/400°F/ Gas 6. Line several baking sheets with non-stick baking paper. Sift the flour into a mixing bowl and add the salt, pepper and mustard. Cut the butter into pieces and rub into the flour mixture until it resembles fine breadcrumbs. Use a fork to stir in the cheese and egg, and mix together to form a soft dough. Knead lightly on a floured surface and cut into 4 equal pieces.

2 Knead chopped nuts into one piece, dill seeds into another piece and curry paste and chilli sauce into each of the remaining pieces. Wrap each piece of flavoured dough in clear film and leave to chill in the fridge for at least an hour. Remove from the clear film and roll out one piece at a time.

3 Using different shaped cutters, stamp out about 20 shapes from each piece. Arrange the shapes on the baking sheets and bake in the oven for 6–8 minutes or until slightly puffed up and pale gold in colour. Cool on wire racks, then remove the biscuits from the baking sheets, using a palette knife.

Tapas of Almonds, Olives and Cheese

These three simple ingredients are lightly flavoured to create a delicious Spanish tapas medley

that is perfect for a casual starter or nibbles to serve with pre-dinner drinks.

INGREDIENTS

2.5ml/½ tsp coriander seeds
2.5ml/½ tsp fennel seeds
5ml/1 tsp chopped fresh rosemary
10ml/2 tsp chopped fresh parsley
2 garlic cloves, crushed
15ml/1 tbsp sherry vinegar
30ml/2 tbsp olive oil
115g/4oz/⅔ cup black olives
115g/4oz/⅔ cup green olives

For the Marinated Cheese
150g/5oz goat's cheese
90ml/6 tbsp olive oil
15ml/1 tbsp white wine vinegar
5ml/1 tsp black peppercorns
1 garlic clove, sliced
3 fresh tarragon or thyme sprigs
tarragon sprigs, to garnish

For the Salted Almonds
1.5ml/¼ tsp cayenne pepper
30ml/2 tbsp sea salt
25g/1oz/2 tbsp butter
60ml/4 tbsp olive oil
200g/7oz/1¾ cups blanched almonds
extra sea salt for sprinkling (optional)

Serves 6–8

COOK'S TIP

If serving with pre-dinner drinks, provide cocktail sticks for spearing the olives and cheese.

1 To make the marinated olives, crush the coriander and fennel seeds with a pestle and mortar. Or, put them into a strong plastic bag and crush them with a rolling pin. Mix together with the rosemary, parsley, garlic, vinegar and oil and pour over the olives in a small bowl. Cover with clear film and chill for up to 1 week.

2 To make the marinated cheese, cut the cheese into bite-size pieces, leaving the rind on. Mix together the oil, vinegar, peppercorns, garlic and herb sprigs and pour over the cheese in a small bowl. Cover with clear film and chill for up to 3 days.

3 To make the salted almonds, mix together the cayenne pepper and salt in a large mixing bowl. Melt the butter with the olive oil in a frying pan. Add the almonds to the frying pan and stir-fry for about 5 minutes, until the almonds are golden.

4 Tip the almonds out of the frying pan, into the salt mixture, and toss together until the almonds are coated. Leave to cool, then remove with a slotted spoon and store them in a jar or airtight container for up to 1 week.

5 To serve the tapas, arrange in small, shallow serving dishes. Use fresh sprigs of tarragon to garnish the cheese and scatter the almonds with a little more salt, if desired.

GUACAMOLE

This fiery version of a popular Mexican dish always proves a favourite at parties. The dip can be served with any number of accompaniments, including tortilla chips, crudités or breadsticks.

INGREDIENTS

2 ripe avocados, peeled and stoned
2 tomatoes, peeled, seeded and finely chopped
6 spring onions, finely chopped
1–2 chillies, seeded and finely chopped
30ml/2 tbsp fresh lime or lemon juice
15ml/1 tbsp chopped fresh coriander
salt and freshly ground black pepper
coriander sprigs, to garnish

Serves 4

1 Put the avocado halves into a large mixing bowl and mash them roughly with a large fork.

2 Add the remaining ingredients. Mix well and season according to taste. Serve garnished with fresh coriander.

COOK'S TIP

When preparing chillies, always be sure to wash your hands immediately after slicing them. The oils released can burn if you accidentally touch your face or eyes. If you have sensitive skin, it is a good idea to wear a pair of plastic gloves.

Prawn Toasts

These crunchy sesame-topped toasts are simple to prepare using a food processor for the prawn paste.

INGREDIENTS

*225g/8oz/2 cups cooked, shelled prawns,
well drained and dried
1 egg white
2 spring onions, chopped
5ml/1 tsp chopped fresh root ginger
1 garlic clove, chopped
5ml/1 tsp cornflour
2.5ml/½ tsp salt
2.5ml/½ tsp sugar
2–3 dashes hot pepper sauce
8 slices firm textured white bread
60–75ml/4–5 tbsp sesame seeds
vegetable oil, for frying
spring onion pompom, to garnish*

Makes 64

COOK'S TIP

You can prepare these toasts in advance and heat them up in a hot oven before serving. Make sure they are crisp and properly heated through – they won't be nearly as enjoyable if there's no crunch.

1 Put the first 9 ingredients in the bowl of a food processor and process until the mixture forms a smooth paste, scraping down the side of the bowl occasionally.

2 Spread the prawn paste evenly over the bread slices, then sprinkle on the sesame seeds, pressing to make them stick. Remove the crusts, then cut each slice diagonally into 4 triangles, then cut each in half again to make 64.

3 Heat 5cm/2in vegetable oil in a heavy saucepan or wok, until hot but not smoking. Fry the triangles for 30–60 seconds, turning once. Drain well and serve hot, garnished with the spring onion pompom.

PASTRY-WRAPPED CHORIZO PUFFS

These flaky pastry puffs, filled with spicy chorizo sausage and grated cheese, make a perfect

accompaniment to a glass of sherry or cold beer at an informal Christmas party.

INGREDIENTS

225g/8oz puff pastry, thawed if frozen
115g/4oz cured chorizo sausage,
chopped
50g/2oz/½ cup grated hard cheese
1 small egg, beaten
5 ml/1 tsp paprika

Serves 8

COOK'S TIP

To prepare the chorizo puffs ahead, chill them without the glaze, wrapped in a plastic bag, until ready to bake, then allow them to come back to room temperature while you preheat the oven. Glaze before baking.

1 Roll out the pastry thinly on a floured surface. Using a 7.5cm/3in cutter, stamp out as many rounds as possible, then re-roll the trimmings, and stamp out more rounds to make 16 in all.

2 Preheat the oven to 220°C/425°F/ Gas 7. Toss the chopped chorizo sausage and grated cheese together.

3 Lay one of the pastry rounds on the palm of your hand and place a little of the chorizo mixture across the centre.

4 Using your other hand, carefully pinch the edges of the pastry together along the top to seal, as when making a miniature pastie. Repeat the process with the remaining rounds to make 16 puffs in all. Place the pastries on a non-stick baking sheet as you work.

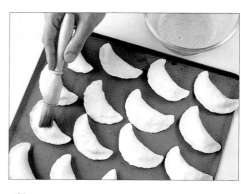

5 Lightly brush each of the pastries with the beaten egg to glaze. Using a small sieve or tea strainer, dust the tops lightly with a little of the paprika.

6 Bake the pastries in the preheated oven for 10–12 minutes, until they are puffed and golden brown. Transfer the pastries to a wire rack and leave them to cool for about 5 minutes, then serve them warm, dusted with the rest of the paprika.

Hot Salt Beef on a Stick

Because this nibble-on-a-stick is so quick to make, it makes an excellent choice for a party.

INGREDIENTS

vegetable oil, for frying
unsliced rye bread with caraway seeds,
cut into 24 x 1cm/½in cubes
225g/8oz salt beef or pastrami, in one
piece
mild mustard, for spreading
2 pickled cucumbers, cut into small pieces
24 cocktail onions

Makes 24

COOK'S TIP

For a more traditionally English version of the same dish, use cubes of thick white bread threaded on cocktail sticks with salt beef or smoked ham and pickled onions, and served with horseradish sauce.

1 In a heavy medium-sized frying pan, heat 1cm/½in of oil. When very hot, but not smoking, add half the bread cubes and fry for about 1 minute until just golden, turning occasionally. Remove the cubes with a slotted spoon and drain them on kitchen paper. Repeat with the remaining cubes.

2 Cut the salt beef or pastrami into 1cm/½in cubes on a chopping board, and spread one side of each cube with a little of the mustard.

3 Thread a bread cube on to a cocktail stick, then a piece of meat with the mustard side against the bread, then a piece of pickled cucumber, and finally an onion. Arrange the cocktail sticks on a plate or tray, and serve immediately.

Lamb Tikka

Creamy yogurt and nuts go wonderfully with the spices in these little Indian meatballs.

Ingredients

450g/1lb lamb fillet
2 spring onions, chopped

For the Marinade
350ml/12fl oz/1½ cups natural yogurt
15ml/1 tbsp ground almonds, cashews or peanuts
15ml/1 tbsp vegetable oil
2–3 garlic cloves, finely chopped
juice of 1 lemon
5ml/1 tsp garam masala or curry powder
2.5ml/½ tsp ground cardamom
1.5ml/¼ tsp cayenne pepper
15–30ml/1–2 tbsp chopped fresh mint

Makes about 20

1 Prepare the marinade. In a medium-size bowl, stir together all the ingredients. In a separate small bowl, reserve about 120ml/4fl oz/½ cup of the mixture to use as a dipping sauce.

2 Cut the lamb into small pieces and put in a food processor with the spring onions. Process until the meat is finely chopped. Add 30–45ml/2–3 tbsp of the marinade and process again.

3 Test to see if the mixture holds together by pinching a little between your fingertips. Add a little more marinade if necessary, but do not make the mixture too wet and soft.

4 With moistened palms, form the meat mixture into slightly oval-shaped balls about 4cm/1½in long and arrange in a shallow baking dish. Spoon over the remaining marinade and refrigerate the meat balls for 8–10 hours or overnight.

5 Preheat the grill and line a baking sheet with foil. Thread each meatball on to a skewer and arrange on the baking sheet. Grill for 4–5 minutes, turning occasionally, until crisp and golden on all sides. Serve with the reserved marinade/dipping sauce.

CHICKEN SATAY WITH PEANUT SAUCE

These skewers of marinated chicken can be prepared in advance and served at room temperature.

Beef, pork or even lamb fillet can be used instead of chicken, if you prefer.

INGREDIENTS

450g/1lb boneless, skinless chicken breasts
sesame seeds, for sprinkling
red pepper, to garnish

For the Marinade
90ml/6 tbsp vegetable oil
60ml/4 tbsp tamari or light soy sauce
60ml/4 tbsp fresh lime juice
2.5cm/1in piece fresh root ginger, peeled and chopped
3–4 garlic cloves
30ml/2 tbsp soft light brown sugar
5ml/1 tsp Chinese-style chilli sauce or 1 small red chilli pepper, seeded and chopped
30ml/2 tbsp chopped fresh coriander

For the Peanut Sauce
30ml/2 tbsp smooth peanut butter
30ml/2 tbsp soy sauce
15ml/1 tbsp sesame or vegetable oil
2 spring onions, chopped
2 garlic cloves
15–30ml/1–2 tbsp fresh lime or lemon juice
15ml/1 tbsp soft light brown sugar

Makes about 24

1 Prepare the marinade. Place all the marinade ingredients in the bowl of a food processor or blender and process until smooth and well blended, scraping down sides of the bowl once. Pour into a shallow dish and set aside.

2 Into the same food processor or blender, put all the peanut sauce ingredients and process until well blended. If the sauce is too thick, add a little water and process again. Pour the sauce into a small bowl and cover until ready to serve.

3 Put the chicken breasts in the freezer for about 5 minutes to firm. On a chopping board, slice the chicken breasts in half horizontally, then cut them into thin strips. Cut the strips into 2cm/¾in pieces.

4 Add the chicken pieces to the marinade in the dish. Toss the chicken well to coat, cover with clear film and marinate for 3–4 hours in a cool place, or overnight in a refrigerator.

5 Preheat the grill. Line a baking sheet with foil and brush lightly with oil. Thread 2–3 pieces of marinated chicken on to skewers and sprinkle with the sesame seeds. Grill for 4–5 minutes until golden, turning once. Serve with the peanut sauce and a garnish of red pepper strips.

Spicy Sun-dried Tomato Pizza Wedges

These spicy pizza wedges can be made with or without the pepperoni or sausage.

INGREDIENTS

45–60ml/3–4 tbsp olive oil
2 onions, thinly sliced
2 garlic cloves, chopped
225g/8oz mushrooms, sliced
225g/8oz can chopped tomatoes
225g/8oz pepperoni or cooked Italian-style
spicy sausage, chopped
5ml/1 tsp chilli flakes
5ml/1 tsp dried oregano
115g/4oz sun-dried tomatoes, packed in oil,
drained and sliced
450g/1lb bottled marinated artichoke
hearts, well drained and cut into quarters
225g/8oz mozzarella cheese, shredded
60ml/4 tbsp freshly grated Parmesan cheese
fresh basil leaves, stoned black olives and
sliced fresh red pepper, to garnish

For the Dough
1 packet pizza dough mix
cornmeal, for dusting
virgin olive oil, for brushing and drizzling

Makes 32

1 Prepare the pizza dough according to the manufacturer's instructions on the packet. Set the prepared dough aside to rise for the required amount of time.

2 Prepare the tomato sauce. In a large deep frying pan, heat the oil over medium-high heat. Add the sliced onions and cook for 3–5 minutes until softened. Add the chopped garlic and mushrooms and cook for 3–4 minutes more, until the mushrooms begin to change colour.

3 Stir in the chopped tomatoes, pepperoni or sausage, chilli flakes and oregano and simmer for 20–30 minutes, stirring frequently, until the sauce is thickened and reduced. Stir in the sun-dried tomatoes and set the sauce aside to cool slightly.

4 Preheat the oven to 240°C/475°F/ Gas 9. Line 1 large or 2 small baking sheets with foil, shiny side up. Sprinkle generously with cornmeal. Cut the dough in half and roll out each half to a 30cm/ 12in round. Transfer to the baking sheet and brush the dough with oil.

5 Divide the spicy tomato sauce between the dough rounds, spreading to within 1cm/½in of the edge. Bake in the preheated oven for 5 minutes, on the lowest shelf of the oven. Arrange half the artichoke hearts over each dough round, sprinkle evenly with the mozzarella and a little Parmesan. Bake each one in the oven on the bottom shelf for 12–15 minutes longer, until the edge of the crust is crisp and brown and the topping is golden and bubbling. Transfer the pizza rounds on to a wire rack, using a palette knife, and allow to cool slightly.

6 Slide the pizzas on to a chopping board and cut each into 16 thin wedges. Garnish each pizza wedge with a basil leaf, one black olive and a slice of pepper and serve immediately.

BLINIS WITH SMOKED SALMON AND DILL CREAM

This recipe is perfect for New Year's Eve celebrations. The blinis go well with a glass of sparkling wine.

INGREDIENTS

115g/4oz/scant cup buckwheat flour
115g/4oz/1 cup plain flour
pinch of salt
15ml/1 tbsp easy-blend dried yeast
2 eggs
350ml/12fl oz/1½ cups warm milk
15g/½oz/1 tbsp melted butter,
150ml/¼ pint/⅔ cup crème fraîche
45ml/3 tbsp chopped fresh dill
225g/8oz smoked salmon, thinly sliced
fresh dill sprigs, to garnish

Serves 4

1 Mix together the flours in a large bowl with salt. Sprinkle in the yeast and mix. Separate one egg. Whisk together the whole egg and the yolk, the warmed milk and the melted butter.

2 Pour the egg mixture on to the flour mixture. Beat well to form a smooth batter. Cover with clear film and leave to rise for 1–2 hours.

3 Whisk the remaining egg white until it holds stiff peaks, and fold into the batter.

4 Preheat a heavy-based frying pan or griddle and brush with melted butter. Drop tablespoons of the batter on to the pan, spacing them well apart. Cook for about 40 seconds, until bubbles appear on the surface.

5 Flip over the blinis and cook for 30 seconds on the other side. Wrap in foil and keep warm in a low oven. Repeat with the remaining mixture, buttering the pan each time.

6 Mix together the crème fraîche and the chopped fresh dill. Serve the blinis topped with the slices of smoked salmon and the dill cream. Garnish each of the blinis with sprigs of fresh dill before serving.

Parmesan Filo Triangles

You can whip up these light and crunchy triangles at the last minute, using fresh or frozen sheets of filo pastry.

INGREDIENTS

3 large sheets filo pastry
olive oil, for brushing
45–60ml/3–4 tbsp freshly grated
Parmesan cheese
2.5ml/½ tsp crumbled dried thyme or sage

Makes about 24

COOK'S TIP

These will keep in an airtight container for up to three days, but handle carefully as they are very fragile. Reheat the triangles in a moderate oven to crisp them up when you are ready to serve them.

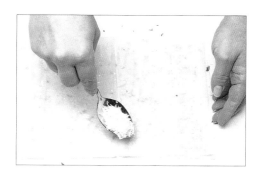

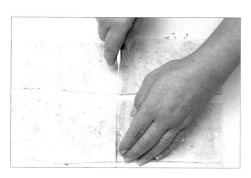

1 Preheat the oven to 180°C/350°F/ Gas 4. Line a large baking sheet with foil and brush lightly with oil. Lay one sheet of filo pastry on a work surface and brush lightly with a little olive oil. Sprinkle lightly with half the Parmesan cheese and a little of the crumbled dried thyme or sage.

2 Cover with a second sheet of filo, brush with a little more oil and sprinkle with the remaining cheese and thyme or sage. Top with the remaining sheet of filo and brush very lightly with a little more oil. With a sharp knife, cut the filo pastry stack in half lengthways and then into squares. Cut each square into triangles.

3 Arrange the triangles on the baking sheet, scrunching them up slightly. Do not allow them to touch. Bake for 6–8 minutes until crisp and golden. Cool slightly and serve immediately.

MINI FILLED JACKET POTATOES

Jacket potatoes are always delicious, and the toppings can easily be varied: choose from luxurious

and extravagant ingredients, such as caviar and smoked salmon, to equally satisfying,

but more everyday fare, such as cheese and baked beans.

INGREDIENTS

*36 potatoes, about 4cm/1½in in diameter,
well scrubbed
250ml/8fl oz/1 cup thick soured cream
45–60ml/3–4 tbsp snipped fresh chives
coarse salt, for sprinkling*

Makes 36

COOK'S TIP

*The potatoes can be baked in
advance in the oven, then reheated
in the microwave on high (100%)
for 3–4 minutes.*

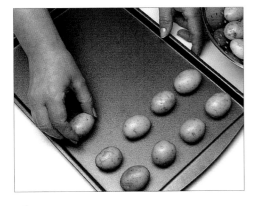

1 Preheat the oven to 180°C/350°F/
Gas 4. Place the potatoes on a baking
sheet and bake in the oven for 30–
35 minutes, or until the potatoes are
tender when pierced with the tip of
a sharp kitchen knife.

2 To serve, make a cross in the top
of each potato and squeeze gently to
open. Make a hole in the centre of
each potato. Fill each one with soured
cream, then sprinkle with the salt and
the snipped chives. Serve immediately.

VARIATION

*If your guests are likely to be
hungry, use medium-size potatoes.
When cooked, cut in half, scoop out
the flesh, mash with the other
ingredients and spoon the mixture
back into the skin. Serve warm.*

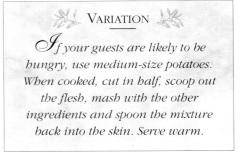

Filo Crackers

These festive-shaped sweet treats will make any party go with a bang! The crackers can be

prepared a day in advance, brushed with melted butter and kept covered with clear film

in the fridge or freezer before baking.

INGREDIENTS

2 x 275g/10oz packet frozen filo pastry,
thawed
115g/4oz/½ cup butter, melted
thin foil ribbon, to decorate
sifted icing sugar, to decorate

For the Filling
450g/1lb eating apples, peeled, cored and
finely chopped
5ml/1 tsp ground cinnamon
25g/1oz/2 tbsp soft light brown sugar
50g/2oz/½ cup chopped pecan nuts
50g/2oz/1 cup fresh white breadcrumbs
25g/1oz/3 tbsp sultanas
25g/1oz/3 heaped tbsp currants

For the Lemon Sauce
115g/4oz/⅔ cup caster sugar
finely grated rind of 1 lemon
juice of 2 lemons

Makes about 24

2 Take one sheet of pastry at a time and cut it into 15 x 30cm/6 x 12in strips. Brush with butter. Place a spoonful of the filling at one end and fold in the sides, so the pastry measures 13cm/5in across. Brush the edges with the melted butter and roll up. Pinch the "frill" tightly at either end of the cracker. Brush once again with melted butter.

4 To make the lemon sauce, put all the ingredients in a small saucepan and heat gently until all of the ingredients are dissolved, stirring occasionally. Pour the warm sauce into a sauce boat and serve with the filo crackers.

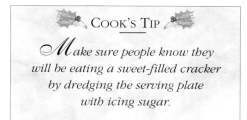

🌿 COOK'S TIP 🌿

Make sure people know they will be eating a sweet-filled cracker by dredging the serving plate with icing sugar.

1 Unwrap the filo pastry and cover it with clear film and a damp cloth, to prevent it from drying out. Put the chopped apples in a large bowl and mix in the remaining filling ingredients.

3 Place the crackers on baking trays, cover and chill for 10 minutes. Preheat the oven to 190°C/375°F/Gas 5. Brush each cracker with melted butter. Bake the crackers for 30–35 minutes, or until they are golden brown. Let them cool slightly on the baking trays and then transfer them to a wire rack to allow them to cool completely.

Sablés with Goat's Cheese and Strawberries

Sablés are little French biscuits. They contrast well with the cheese and fruit in this recipe

and taste great served with a glass of chilled white wine.

Ingredients

75g/3oz/6 tbsp butter, at room temperature
140g/5oz/1 generous cup plain flour
75g/3oz/6 tbsp blanched hazelnuts, lightly toasted and ground
30ml/2 tbsp caster sugar
2 egg yolks beaten with 30–45ml/ 2–3 tbsp water
115g/4oz goat's cheese
4–6 large strawberries, cut into small pieces
chopped hazelnuts, to decorate

Makes about 24

1 Make the pastry. Put the butter, flour, ground hazelnuts, sugar and beaten egg yolks into a food processor and process to make a smooth dough.

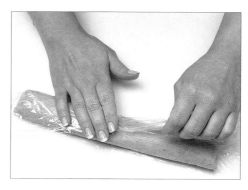

2 Put the dough on to clear film and use the film to shape it into a log 4cm/ 1½in in diameter. Wrap and refrigerate overnight until very firm.

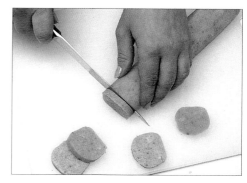

3 Preheat the oven to 200°C/400°F/ Gas 6 and line a large baking sheet with non-stick baking paper. Slice the dough into 5mm/¼in thick rounds and arrange on the baking sheet. Bake for 7–10 minutes until golden brown. Remove to a wire rack to cool.

4 Crumble the cheese into pieces and mound a little on each sablé. Top with strawberry and sprinkle with hazelnuts. Serve warm.

Variation

*B*eat 75g/3oz cream cheese with 15ml/1 tbsp icing sugar and a little lemon zest. Spread on top of the sablé and top with any sliced fruits.

RICH CHOCOLATE AND FRUIT FONDUE

This sumptuous fruit fondue, with its rich, delicious sauce, makes a lavish finale to a party menu.

INGREDIENTS

*a selection of mixed fruit, such as
kumquats, apples, peaches and pears,
bananas, clementines, seedless grapes,
cherries, lychees, mango and papaya,
figs, plums and strawberries
lemon juice*

For the Chocolate
*225g/8oz good quality plain chocolate,
chopped
30ml/2 tbsp golden syrup
120ml/4fl oz/½ cup whipping cream
30–45ml/2–3 tbsp brandy or
orange liqueur*

Makes 350ml/12fl oz/1½ cups

2 In a pan over a low heat, combine the chocolate, golden syrup and cream. Stir until the chocolate is melted and smooth. Remove from the heat and stir in the brandy or liqueur. Pour into a serving bowl and serve with the fruit.

VARIATION

You could also use small biscuits, such as langues de chat or amaretti for dipping as well as, or instead of, the assorted pieces of fresh fruit.

1 On a chopping board, cut the kumquats, apples, peaches, pears and bananas into slices. Break the clementines into segments and peel the lychees, cube the mango and papaya and then cut the figs and plums into wedges. Leave the strawberries whole. Arrange the fruits in an attractive pattern on a large serving dish. Brush any cut-up fruit such as apples, pears or bananas with lemon juice to prevent the pieces from discolouring. Cover the dish with clear film and refrigerate until ready to serve.

Stuffings, Sauces & Preserves

*S*tuffings and sauces make up an essential part
of the Christmas fare but they often require plenty
of preparation time: many cooks find that, if they
don't forget about them altogether amid the hustle and
bustle of the main events, they decide against them as
an optional extra. It is a good idea to tackle as much
as possible in advance. Many of the recipes here improve
with keeping and most can be stored in the fridge or
freezer until they are needed. In the weeks leading up
to Christmas, make the best use of the seasonal produce
available by bottling and preserving it in jars for use
throughout the festive weeks.

Apricot and Raisin Stuffing

Ingredients

40 g/1½oz/3 tbsp butter
1 large onion, sliced
100g/4oz/1 cup dried apricot pieces,
soaked and drained
100g/4oz/⅔ cup seedless raisins
juice and grated rind of 1 orange
1 cooking apple, peeled, cored and
chopped
100g/4oz/2 cups fresh white
breadcrumbs
1.5ml/¼ tsp ground ginger
salt and freshly ground black pepper

Makes about 400g/14oz

1 Heat the butter in a small pan and fry the onion over a moderate heat until it is translucent.

2 Turn the onion into a large mixing bowl and stir in the dried apricots, raisins, orange juice and rind, chopped apple, breadcrumbs and ground ginger.

3 Season with salt and black pepper. Mix well with a wooden spoon, then allow to cool. Use the stuffing to pack the neck end of the bird.

Chestnut Stuffing

Ingredients

40g/1½oz/3 tbsp butter
1 large onion, chopped
450g/1lb can unsweetened chestnut purée
50g/2oz/1 cup fresh white breadcrumbs
45ml/3 tbsp orange juice
grated nutmeg
½ tsp caster sugar
salt and freshly ground black pepper

Makes about 400g/14oz

1 Heat the butter in a saucepan and fry the onion over a moderate heat for about 3 minutes until it is translucent.

2 Remove the saucepan from the heat and mix the onion with the chestnut purée, breadcrumbs, orange juice, grated nutmeg and sugar.

3 Season with salt and ground black pepper. Allow to cool. Use the stuffing to pack the neck end of the turkey.

Cranberry and Rice Stuffing

Ingredients

225g/8oz/1¼ cups long grain rice, washed
and drained
600ml/1 pint/2½ cups meat or poultry
stock
50g/2oz/4 tbsp butter
1 large onion, chopped
150g/6oz/1 cup cranberries
60ml/4 tbsp orange juice
15ml/1 tbsp chopped parsley
10ml/2 tsp chopped thyme
grated nutmeg
salt and freshly ground black pepper

Makes about 450g/1lb

1 Boil the rice and stock in a small pan. Cover and simmer for 15 minutes. Tip the rice into a bowl and set aside. Heat the butter in a small pan and fry the onion. Add it to the rice.

2 Put the cranberries and orange juice in the cleaned pan and simmer until the fruit is tender. Tip the fruit and any remaining juice into the rice.

3 Add the herbs and season. Allow to cool. Use to pack the turkey neck.

Clockwise from top: Chestnut Stuffing, Cranberry and Rice Stuffing, Apricot and Raisin Stuffing.

Apricot and Orange Stuffing

INGREDIENTS

15g/½oz/1 tbsp butter
1 small onion, finely chopped
115g/4oz/2 cups fresh breadcrumbs
50g/2oz/¼ cup finely chopped dried apricots
grated rind of ½ orange
1 small egg, beaten
15ml/1 tbsp chopped fresh parsley
salt and freshly ground black pepper

Makes about 400g/14oz

1 Heat the butter in a frying pan and cook the onion gently until tender.

2 Allow to cool slightly, and add the onion to the rest of the ingredients.

3 Mix until thoroughly combined and season with plenty of salt and pepper.

Parsley, Lemon and Thyme Stuffing

INGREDIENTS

115g/4oz/2 cups fresh breadcrumbs
25g/1oz/2 tbsp butter
25g/1 tbsp chopped fresh parsley
2.5ml/½ tsp dried thyme
grated rind of ¼ lemon
1 rasher streaky bacon, chopped
1 small egg, beaten
salt and freshly ground black pepper

Makes about 400g/14oz

1 Mix all the ingredients together in a large bowl and stir to combine them thoroughly.

Raisin and Nut Stuffing

INGREDIENTS

115g/4oz/2 cups fresh breadcrumbs
50g/2oz/⅓ cup raisins
50g/2oz/½ cup walnuts, almonds, pistachios or pine nuts
15ml/1 tbsp chopped fresh parsley
5ml/1 tsp chopped mixed herbs
1 small egg, beaten
25g/1oz/2 tbsp melted butter
salt and freshly ground black pepper

Makes about 400g/14oz

1 Mix all the ingredients together thoroughly. Season well with plenty of salt and ground black pepper.

BREAD SAUCE

Smooth and surprisingly delicate, this old-fashioned sauce is traditionally served with roast

chicken, turkey and game birds. If you'd prefer a less strong flavour, reduce the number

of cloves and add a little freshly grated nutmeg instead.

INGREDIENTS

1 small onion
4 cloves
bay leaf
300ml/½ pint/1¼ cup milk
115g/4oz/2 cups fresh white breadcrumbs
15ml/1 tbsp butter
15ml/1 tbsp light cream
salt and freshly ground black pepper

Serves 6

1 Peel the onion and stick the cloves into it. Put it into a saucepan with the bay leaf and pour in the milk.

2 Bring to the boil then remove from the heat and steep for 15–20 minutes. Remove the bay leaf and onion.

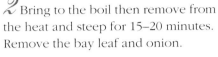

3 Return to the heat and stir in the crumbs. Simmer for 4–5 minutes or until thick and creamy.

4 Stir in the butter and cream. Season with salt and pepper and serve.

CRANBERRY SAUCE

This is the sauce for roast turkey, but don't just keep it for festive occasions. The vibrant colour and tart taste

are perfect partners for any white roast meat, and it makes a great addition to a chicken sandwich.

INGREDIENTS

1 orange
225g/8oz/2 cups cranberries
250g/9oz/1¼ cups sugar

Serves 6

1 Pare the rind thinly from the orange, taking care not to remove any white pith. Squeeze the juice.

2 Place the orange rind in a saucepan with the cranberries, sugar and 150 ml/¼ pint/⅔ cup water.

3 Bring to the boil, stirring until the sugar has dissolved, then simmer for 10–15 minutes or until the berries burst.

4 Remove the rind. Cool before serving.

Tartare Sauce

This is an authentic tartare sauce to serve with all kinds of fish, but for a simpler version

you could always stir the flavourings into mayonnaise.

INGREDIENTS

2 hard-boiled eggs
1 egg yolk from a large egg
10ml/2 tsp lemon juice
175ml/6fl oz/¾ cup olive oil
5ml/1 tsp chopped capers
5ml/1 tsp chopped gherkins
5ml/1 tsp chopped fresh chives
5ml/1 tsp chopped fresh parsley
salt and white pepper

Serves 6

1 Halve the hard-boiled eggs, remove the yolks and press them through a strainer into a mixing bowl.

2 Using a spatula, blend in the raw yolk and mix thoroughly until smooth. Stir in the lemon juice.

3 Add the oil very slowly, a little at a time, whisking constantly. When it begins to thicken, add the oil more quickly to form a thick emulsion. Use a hand blender (mixer) if you prefer.

4 Finely chop one egg white and stir into the sauce with the capers, gherkins and herbs. Season to taste. Serve as an accompaniment to fried or grilled fish.

Mousseline Sauce

This truly luscious sauce is subtly flavoured, rich and creamy. Serve it as a dip with prepared

artichokes or artichoke hearts, or with fish or poultry goujons.

INGREDIENTS

1 quantity Hollandaise sauce
or for a less rich sauce:
2 egg yolks
15ml/1 tbsp lemon juice
75g/3oz/6 tbsp softened butter
90ml/6 tbsp double cream
salt and freshly ground black pepper

Serves 4

3 Using a large balloon whisk, whisk the double cream in a bowl. Continue to whisk the mixture until stiff peaks form.

4 Fold into the warm Hollandaise or prepared sauce and adjust the seasoning. You can add a little more lemon juice for extra tang.

1 If you are not using prepared Hollandaise, make the sauce: whisk the yolks and lemon juice in a bowl over a pan of barely simmering water until very thick and fluffy.

2 Whisk in the softened butter, adding only a very little at a time; whisk well until it is thoroughly absorbed and the sauce has the consistency of mayonnaise.

Crème Anglais

Here is the classic English custard; it is light and creamy without the harsh flavours

or gaudy colouring of its poorer package relations. Serve hot or cold.

INGREDIENTS

1 vanilla pod
450ml/15fl oz/1⅞ cups milk
40g/1½oz/3 tbsp icing sugar
4 egg yolks

Serves 4

VARIATION

Steep a few strips of thinly pared lemon or orange rind with the milk, instead of the vanilla pod.

1 Put the vanilla pod in a saucepan with the milk. Bring slowly to the boil. Remove from the heat and steep for 10 minutes before removing the pod.

2 Beat together the sugar and egg yolk until thick, light and creamy.

3 Slowly pour the warm milk on to the egg mixture, stirring constantly.

4 Place the bowl over a saucepan of hot water. Stir over a low heat for 10 minutes or until the mixture coats the back of the spoon. Remove from the heat immediately as curdling will occur if the custard is allowed to simmer.

5 Strain the custard into a jug if serving hot or, if serving cold, strain into a bowl and cover the surface with buttered paper or clear film.

CUMBERLAND RUM BUTTER

No Christmas Dinner would be complete without a traditional Christmas pudding to round it off.

This rich and luscious rum butter is the perfect accompaniment.

INGREDIENTS

225g/8oz/1 cup unsalted butter at room temperature
225g/8oz/1 cup soft light brown sugar
90ml/6 tbsp dark rum, or to taste

Makes about 450g/1lb

1 Beat the butter and sugar until the mixture is soft, creamy and pale in colour. Gradually add the rum, almost drop by drop, beating to incorporate each addition before adding more. If you are too hasty in adding the rum, the mixture may curdle.

2 When all the rum has been added, spoon the mixture into a covered container and chill for at least 1 hour. The butter will keep well in the fridge for about 4 weeks.

VARIATION

A variety of liqueurs can be added to the butter and sugar to make delicious alternative accompaniments. Try the recipe with brandy or an orange-flavoured liqueur.

Savoury Butters

This selection of 8 tiny pots of unusual flavoured butters can be used as garnishes for meat,

fish and vegetables, as a topping for canapés or as a tasty addition to sauces.

INGREDIENTS

450g/1lb/2 cups unsalted butter
25g/1oz/2 tbsp Stilton
3 anchovy fillets
5ml/1 tsp curry paste
1 garlic clove, crushed
10g/2 tsp finely chopped fresh tarragon
15ml/1 tbsp creamed horseradish
15ml/1 tbsp chopped fresh parsley
5ml/1 tsp grated lime rind
1.5ml/¼ tsp chilli sauce

Makes about 50g/2oz/¼ cup
of each flavour

1 Place the butter in a food processor. Process until light and fluffy. Divide the butter into 8 portions.

2 Crumble the Stilton and mix together with a portion of butter. Pound the anchovies to a paste with a mortar and pestle and mix with the second portion of butter. Stir the curry paste into the third and the crushed garlic into the fourth portion.

3 Stir the tarragon into the fifth portion and the creamed horseradish into the sixth portion. Into the seventh portion add the parsley and the lime rind, and to the last portion add the chilli sauce. Pack each flavoured butter into a tiny sterilized jar with a lid and label clearly. Store in the fridge.

COOK'S TIP

Make up a whole batch of these butters and freeze them. They will keep unopened in the freezer for up to 3 months. Once opened, consume within 3 days.

Anchovy Spread

This delicious spread has an intense concentrated flavour and is best served with plain toast.

INGREDIENTS

*2 x 50g/2oz cans anchovy
fillets in olive oil
4 garlic cloves, crushed
2 egg yolks
30ml/2 tbsp red wine vinegar
300ml/½ pint/1¼ cups olive oil
1.5ml/¼ tsp freshly ground black pepper
30ml/2 tbsp chopped fresh basil or thyme*

Makes 600ml/1 pint/2½ cups

1 Drain the oil from the anchovies and reserve. Place the anchovies and garlic in a food processor. Process until smooth. Add the egg yolks and vinegar, and process until the egg and vinegar have been absorbed by the anchovies.

2 Measure out the oil into a measuring jug and add the reserved anchovy oil. Set the food processor to a low speed and gradually add the oil, drop by drop, to the anchovy mixture until it is thick and smooth.

3 Add some freshly ground black pepper and the chopped fresh herbs, and blend well until the mixture is smooth. Spoon the mixture into small sterilized jars with lids, seal with a wax paper disc, cover with the lid, and label with the name of the spread and the date it was made. Store the unopened jars of spread in the fridge until it is needed.

CHRISTMAS CHUTNEY

This chutney makes the perfect accompaniment to cold meats, pâtés and cheese. It has a sweet

but spicy flavour. The fruits may be changed for quince, greengage or rhubarb.

INGREDIENTS

450g/1lb/9 plums, stoned
450g/1lb/6 pears, peeled and cored
225g/8oz/2 cooking apples, peeled and cored
225g/8oz/4 sticks celery
450g/1lb onions, sliced
450g/1 lb tomatoes, skinned
115g/4oz/⅔ cup raisins
15ml/1 tbsp grated fresh root ginger
30ml/2 tbsp pickling spice
850ml/1½ pints/3¾ cups cider vinegar
450g/1lb/2 cups granulated sugar

Makes 1.75kg/4¼lb

1 Chop the plums, pears, apples, celery and onions and cut the tomatoes into quarters. Place all these ingredients with the raisins and ginger into a very large saucepan.

2 Place the pickling spice into a square of clean, fine muslin and tie with string to secure. Add to the saucepan of fruit and vegetables with half the vinegar and bring to the boil, stirring. Cook for 2 hours.

3 Meanwhile, sterilize the jars and lids you will need to fill. When all the ingredients are tender, stir in the remaining vinegar and the sugar. Boil until thick, remove the bag of spices and fill each jar with chutney. Cover with a wax paper disc and plastic lid, and label when cold.

COOK'S TIP

Once opened, this chutney will keep for up to one week in a resealable jar. If you wish, add attractive ribbons, tags and labels and give it to a friend as a special Christmas gift.

PICCALILLI

The piquancy of this relish partners well with sausages, as well as with most bacon or ham dishes.

INGREDIENTS

675g/1½lb cauliflower
450g/1lb small onions
350g/12oz French beans
5ml/1 tsp ground turmeric
5ml/1 tsp dry mustard powder
10ml/2 tsp cornflour
600ml/1 pint/2½ cups vinegar

Makes 3 x 450g/1lb jars

1 Cut the cauliflower into tiny florets.

2 Peel the onions and top and tail the French beans.

3 In a small saucepan, measure in the turmeric, mustard powder and cornflour. Pour the vinegar into the saucepan. Stir well and simmer for 10 minutes over a gentle heat.

4 Pour the vinegar mixture over the vegetables in a large saucepan, mix well and simmer for 45 minutes.

5 Pour into sterilized jars. Seal each jar with a wax disc and a tightly fitting cellophane top. Store in a cool, dark place. The piccalilli will keep well, unopened, for up to a year. Once opened, store in the fridge and consume within a week.

Tomato Chutney

This spicy chutney is delicious with a selection of cheeses and biscuits, or with cold meats.

INGREDIENTS

900g/2lb tomatoes
225g/8oz/1⅓ cups raisins
225g/8oz onions, chopped
225g/8oz/1⅛ cups caster sugar
600ml/1 pint/2½ cups malt vinegar

Makes 3 x 450g/1lb jars

1 Put the tomatoes in a bowl and pour over boiling water. Leave the tomatoes immersed in the water for 30 seconds, then remove with a slotted spoon and plunge them into cold water. Peel the tomatoes and chop roughly. Put in a preserving pan.

2 Add the raisins, chopped onions and caster sugar.

3 Pour over the vinegar. Bring to the boil and let it simmer for 2 hours, uncovered. Pot into sterilized jars. Seal with a wax disc and cover with a tightly fitting cellophane top. Store in a cool, dark place. The chutney will keep well, unopened, for up to a year. Once opened, store in the fridge and consume within a week.

QUINCE PASTE

This paste is known in Spain as pasta de membrillo. *It is decorated with icing sugar and sometimes cloves, and served after meals or to decorate desserts. If you find quinces difficult to get hold of, try using fresh apricots or even cranberries.*

INGREDIENTS

1kg/2¼lb quinces
1 litre/1¾ pints/4 cups water
1kg/2¼lb/4¼ cups caster sugar
vegetable oil, for brushing
icing sugar, for dusting
whole cloves, to decorate

Makes about 1.25kg/2½lb

COOK'S TIP

If you would like to pack this tangy paste as a gift, layer it in a box between sheets of non-stick baking paper.

---

1 Wash and slice the quinces and put them into a large pan with the water. Bring to the boil, then simmer for about 45 minutes, until the fruit is soft.

2 Mash the fruit against the sides of the pan, then spoon it and the liquid into a jelly bag suspended over a large bowl. Leave to drain for at least 2 hours, without squeezing the bag.

3 Pour the strained juice into the cleaned pan, add the sugar and stir over a low heat to dissolve. Cook over a low heat for about 2 hours, stirring frequently, until a spoon drawn through the paste parts it into 2 sections.

4 Lightly brush a Swiss roll tin with oil, pour in the preserve and leave to set. When it is cool, cut it into diamonds or other shapes, dust with icing sugar and stud each piece with a clove. Store between layers of non-stick baking paper in an airtight container.

CRAB-APPLE AND LAVENDER JELLY

This fragrant, clear jelly can be made in the months before Christmas and stored until needed.

INGREDIENTS

900g/2lb/5 cups crab-apples
1.75 litres/3 pints/7½ cups water
lavender stems
900g/2lb/4 cups granulated sugar

Makes about 900g/2lb

1 Cut the crab-apples into chunks and place in a large pan with the water and 2 stems of lavender. Bring to the boil then cover the pan and simmer very gently for 1 hour, stirring occasionally until the fruit is pulpy.

2 Suspend a jelly bag and place a large bowl underneath. Sterilize the jelly bag by pouring through some boiling water. When the bowl is full of water, discard the water and replace the bowl to sit underneath the bag.

3 Pour the pulped fruit mixture from the saucepan slowly into the jelly bag. Allow the juice from the mixture to drip slowly through for several hours. Do not try to speed up the straining process by squeezing the bag or the jelly will become cloudy.

4 Discard the pulp and measure the quantity of juice in the bowl. To each 600ml/1 pint/2½ cups of juice add 450g/1lb/2 cups of sugar and pour into a clean pan. Sterilize the jars and lids required.

5 Heat the juice gently, stirring occasionally, until the sugar has dissolved. Bring to the boil and boil rapidly for about 8–10 minutes until setting point has been reached. When tested, the temperature should be 105°C/221°F. If you don't have a sugar thermometer, put a small amount of jelly on a cold plate and allow to cool. The surface should wrinkle when you push the jelly. If not yet set, continue to boil and then re-test.

6 Remove from the heat and remove any froth from the surface. Pour the jelly into the warm sterilized jars. Dip the lavender into boiling water and insert a stem into each jar. Cover with a disc of wax paper and then with cellophane paper and a rubber band.

Apple and Mint Jelly

This jelly tastes delicious served with freshly cooked vegetables.

It also makes a traditional accompaniment to rich roasted meat such as lamb.

INGREDIENTS

900g/2lb Bramley apples
granulated sugar
45ml/3 tbsp chopped fresh mint

Makes 3 x 450g/1lb jars

1 Chop the apples roughly and put them in a preserving pan.

2 Add enough water to cover the apples. Simmer until the fruit is soft.

3 Suspend a jelly bag and place a bowl underneath. Pour the mixture through the bag, allowing it to drip overnight. Do not squeeze the bag.

4 Measure the amount of juice that drains from the jelly bag. To every 600ml/1 pint/2½ cups of juice, add 500g/1¼lb/2¾ cups granulated sugar. Stir the sugar into the juice.

5 Place the juice and sugar in a large saucepan and warm over a gentle heat, stirring continuously. Dissolve the sugar in the juice and then increase the heat and bring the liquid to the boil. Test for setting by pouring about 15ml/ 1 tbsp onto a cold plate and allowing it to cool. If a wrinkle forms on the surface when pushed with a fingertip, the jelly is almost set. When a set is reached, leave the jelly to cool.

6 Stir in the chopped mint and pot into sterilized jars. Seal each jar with a wax disc and a tightly fitting cellophane top. Store in a cool, dark place. The jelly will keep unopened for up to a year. Once opened, keep in the fridge and consume within a week.

POACHED SPICED PLUMS IN BRANDY

Bottling spiced fruit is a great way to preserve summer flavours for eating in winter.

Serve these spiced plums as a dessert, with freshly whipped cream, if liked.

INGREDIENTS

600ml/1 pint/2½ cups brandy
rind of 1 lemon, peeled in a long strip
350g/12oz/1⅔ cups caster sugar
1 cinnamon stick
900g/2lb fresh plums

Makes 900g/2lb

VARIATION

Other fruits that can be preserved successfully in this way include fresh pears and peaches.

1 Put the brandy, sugar and cinnamon stick in a large pan and heat gently to dissolve the sugar. Add the plums and lemon rind. Poach for 15 minutes, or until soft. Remove with a slotted spoon.

2 Reduce the syrup by a third by rapid boiling. Strain it over the plums. Bottle the plums in large sterilized jars. Seal tightly and store for up to 6 months in a cool, dark place.

Spiced Pickled Pears

These delicious pears are the perfect accompaniment for cooked ham or cold meat salads.

INGREDIENTS

900g/2lb pears
600ml/1 pint/2½ cups white wine vinegar
225g/8oz/1 cup caster sugar
1 cinnamon stick
5 star anise
10 whole cloves

Makes 900g/2lb

COOK'S TIP

The pears will keep for up to a year unopened. Once opened, store in the fridge and consume within one week.

1 Use a sharp knife to peel the pears, keeping them whole and leaving the flesh on the stalks. Heat the white wine vinegar and caster sugar together in a saucepan, stirring continuously, until the sugar has melted. Pour over the pears and poach for 15 minutes.

2 Add the cinnamon stick, star anise and cloves and simmer for 10 minutes. Remove the pears and pack tightly into sterilized jars. Simmer the syrup for a further 15 minutes and strain it over the pears. Seal the jars tightly and store in a cool, dark place.

Puddings & Desserts

Christmas is a time to indulge in puddings and desserts. At Christmas Dinner, most guests will expect Traditional Christmas Pudding, but other variations on the festive theme such as Chocolate and Chestnut Yule Log or Christmas Cranberry Bombe will be just as welcome. After a heavy meal, a fruit-based dessert like Ruby Fruit Salad or Spiced Pears in Red Wine will always be appreciated, and, for successful entertaining, try individual desserts such as sinful Frozen Grand Marnier Soufflés laced with alcohol. Specialities for chocaholics include Amaretto Mousses with Chocolate Sauce, while Chocolate Crêpes with Plums and Port will provide a sophisticated end to any main course dish.

GINGER TRIFLE

This is a good way to use up leftover cake, whether plain, chocolate or gingerbread. You can substitute

runny honey for the ginger and syrup, if you prefer. This pudding can be made the day before.

INGREDIENTS

225g/8oz gingerbread or other cake
60ml/4 tbsp Grand Marnier or sherry
2 ripe dessert pears, peeled, cored and
cubed
2 bananas, thickly sliced
2 oranges, segmented
1–2 pieces stem ginger, finely chopped,
plus 30ml/2 tbsp syrup

For the Custard
2 eggs
50g/2oz/4 tbsp caster sugar
15ml/1 tbsp cornflour
450ml/³⁄₄ pint/1⁷⁄₈ cups milk
few drops vanilla essence

To Decorate
150ml/¹⁄₄ pint/²⁄₃ cup double cream, lightly
whipped
25g/1oz/¹⁄₄ cup chopped almonds, toasted
4 glacé cherries
8 small pieces angelica

Serves 8

3 Mix all the prepared fruit with the ginger and syrup. Spoon into the bowl on top of the gingerbread. Spoon over the custard to cover and chill until set.

4 Cover the top with whipped cream and scatter on the toasted almonds. Arrange the glacé cherries and angelica around the edge.

1 Cut the gingerbread into 4cm/1½in cubes. Put them in the bottom of a 1.75 litre/3 pint/7½ cup glass bowl. Sprinkle over the liqueur and set aside.

2 For the custard, whisk the eggs, sugar and cornflour into a pan with a little milk. Heat the remaining milk until almost boiling. Pour it on to the egg mixture, whisking. Heat, stirring, until thickened. Simmer for 2 minutes. Add the vanilla essence and leave to cool.

Ruby Fruit Salad

After a rich main course, this port-flavoured fruit salad is light and refreshing.

You can use any fruit that is available.

INGREDIENTS

300ml/½ pint/1¼ cups water
115g/4oz/8 tbsp caster sugar
1 cinnamon stick
4 cloves
pared rind of 1 orange
300ml/½ pint/1¼ cups port
2 oranges
1 small ripe Ogen, Charentais or Honeydew melon
4 small bananas
2 dessert apples
225g/8oz seedless grapes

Serves 8

1 Put the water, sugar, spices and pared orange rind into a saucepan and stir, over a gentle heat, to dissolve the sugar. Then bring the liquid to the boil, cover the pan with a lid and allow to simmer gently for 10 minutes. Remove the pan from the heat and set aside to cool, then add the port.

2 Strain the liquid through a sieve into a mixing bowl, to remove the spices and orange rind. With a sharp knife, cut off all the skin and pith from the oranges. Then, holding each orange over the bowl to catch the juice, cut away the segments, by slicing between the membrane that divides each segment and allowing the segments to drop into the syrup. Squeeze the remaining pith to release as much of the remaining juice as possible.

3 On a chopping board, cut the melon in half, remove the seeds and scoop out the flesh with a melon baller, or cut it into small cubes. Add it to the syrup. Peel the bananas and cut them in 1cm/½in slices.

4 Quarter and core the apples and cut them in small cubes. (Leave the skin on or peel if the skin is tough.) Halve the grapes if large, or leave them whole. Stir all the fruit into the syrup, cover and chill for an hour before serving.

Golden Ginger Compote

Warm, spicy and full of sun-ripened ingredients – this is the perfect Christmas dessert.

INGREDIENTS

2 cups kumquats
150g/5oz/1¼ cups dried apricots
25g/1oz/2 tbsp raisins
400ml/14fl oz/1⅔ cups water
1 orange
2.5cm/1in piece fresh root ginger, peeled and grated
4 cardamom pods, crushed
4 cloves
30ml/2 tbsp honey
15g/½oz/1 tbsp slivered almonds, toasted

Serves 4

1 Wash the kumquats, and, if they are large, cut them in half. Place them in a pan with the apricots, raisins and water. Bring to the boil.

2 Pare the rind from the orange and add to the pan. Add the ginger, the cardamom pods and the cloves.

3 Reduce the heat, cover and simmer for about 30 minutes or until the fruit is tender, stirring occasionally.

4 Squeeze the orange juice and add to the pan with honey to sweeten. Sprinkle with almonds and serve.

COOK'S TIP

You can use ready-to-eat dried apricots. Reduce the liquid to 300ml/½ pint/1¼ cups, and add the apricots for the last 5 minutes.

Spiced Pears in Red Wine

Serve these pears hot or cold, with lightly whipped cream. The flavours improve with

keeping, so you can make this several days before you want to serve it.

INGREDIENTS

600ml/1 pint/2½ cups red wine
225g/8oz/1 cup caster sugar
cinnamon stick
6 cloves
finely grated rind of 1 orange
10ml/2 tsp grated root ginger
8 even-sized firm pears, with stalks
15ml/1 tbsp brandy
25g/1oz/2 tbsp almonds or hazelnuts,
toasted, to decorate

Serves 8

3 Remove the pears from the syrup, using a slotted spoon, being careful not to pull out the stalks. Put the pears in one large serving bowl or into 8 individual bowls.

4 Bring the syrup to the boil and boil it rapidly until it thickens and reduces. Allow to cool slightly, add the brandy and strain over the pears. Scatter on the toasted nuts, to decorate.

1 Choose a pan large enough to hold all the pears upright in one layer. Put all the ingredients except the pears, brandy and almonds into the pan and heat slowly until the sugar has dissolved. Simmer for 5 minutes.

2 Peel the pears, leaving the stalks on, and cut away the flower end. Arrange them upright in the pan. Cover with a lid and simmer until they are tender. The cooking time will depend on their size, but will be about 45–50 minutes.

STUFFED PEACHES WITH MASCARPONE CREAM

Mascarpone is a thick, velvety Italian cream cheese, made from cow's milk.

Although it can be used as a thickening agent in savoury recipes, it is often used

in desserts or eaten with a variety of fresh fruit.

INGREDIENTS

4 large peaches, halved and stoned
40g/1½oz amaretti biscuits, crumbled
30ml/2 tbsp ground almonds
45ml/3 tbsp sugar
15ml/1 tbsp cocoa powder
150ml/¼ pint/⅔ cup sweet white wine
25g/1oz/2 tbsp butter

For the Mascarpone Cream
30ml/2 tbsp caster sugar
3 egg yolks
15ml/1 tbsp sweet white wine
225g/8oz/1 cup mascarpone cheese
150ml/¼ pint/⅔ cup double cream

Serves 4

1 Preheat the oven to 200°C/400°F/ Gas 6. Using a teaspoon, scoop some of the flesh from the cavities in the peaches, to make a reasonable space for stuffing. Chop up the scooped-out flesh with a knife.

2 Mix together the amaretti, ground almonds, sugar, cocoa and peach flesh. Add enough wine to make the mixture into a thick paste.

3 Place the halved peaches in a buttered ovenproof dish and fill them with the stuffing. Dot each peach with the butter, then pour the remaining wine into the dish. Bake for 35 minutes.

4 To make the mascarpone cream, beat the sugar and egg yolks until thick and pale. Stir in the wine, then fold in the mascarpone. Whip the double cream to form soft peaks and fold into the mixture. Remove the peaches from the oven and leave to cool. Serve the peaches at room temperature, with the mascarpone.

> ### VARIATION
>
> *As a low-fat alternative to mascarpone cream, mix ½ cup ricotta cheese or fromage frais with 1 tbsp light brown sugar. Spoon the cheese mixture into the hollow of each peach half, using a teaspoon, and sprinkle with a little ground star anise or allspice. Grill for 6–8 minutes and serve.*

CRÊPES WITH ORANGE SAUCE

This is a sophisticated dessert that is easy to make at home. You can make

the crêpes in advance; you will be able to put the dish together quickly at the last minute.

INGREDIENTS

115g/4oz/⅔ cup plain flour
1.5ml/¼ tsp salt
25g/1oz/2 tbsp caster sugar
2 eggs, lightly beaten
250ml/8fl oz/1 cup milk
60ml/4 tbsp water
30ml/2 tbsp orange flower water or orange liqueur (optional)
25g/1oz/2 tbsp unsalted butter, melted, plus more for frying

For the Orange Sauce
75g/3oz/6 tbsp unsalted butter
55g/2oz/¼ cup caster sugar
grated rind and juice of 1 large unwaxed orange
grated rind and juice of 1 unwaxed lemon
150ml/¼ pint/⅔ cup fresh orange juice
60ml/4 tbsp orange liqueur
brandy and orange liqueur, for flaming (optional)
orange segments, to decorate

Serves 6

2 Heat an 18–20cm/7–8in crêpe pan (preferably non-stick) over a medium heat. Stir the melted butter into the crêpe batter. Brush the hot pan with a little extra melted butter and pour in about 30ml/2 tbsp of batter. Quickly tilt and rotate the pan to cover the base with a thin layer of batter. Cook for about 1 minute until the top is set and the base is golden. With a palette knife, lift the edge to check the colour, then carefully turn over the crêpe and cook for 20–30 seconds, just to set. Tip out on to a plate.

4 To make the sauce, melt the butter in a large frying pan over a medium-low heat, then stir in the sugar, orange and lemon rind and juice, the additional orange juice and the orange liqueur, if using.

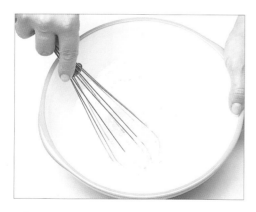

1 Sift together the flour, salt and sugar. Make a well in the centre and pour in the eggs. Beat the eggs, whisking in the flour until it is all incorporated. Whisk in the milk and water until smooth. Whisk in the orange flower water or liqueur. Then strain the batter into a jug and set aside.

3 Continue cooking the crêpes, stirring the batter occasionally and brushing the pan with a little melted butter as and when necessary. Place a sheet of clear film between each crêpe as they are stacked to prevent sticking. (Crêpes can be prepared ahead to this point – wrap and chill until ready to use.)

5 Place a crêpe in the pan browned-side down, swirling gently to coat with the sauce. Fold it in half, then in half again to form a triangle and push to the side of the pan. Continue heating and folding the crêpes until all are warm and covered with the sauce.

6 If you want to flame the crêpes, heat 30–45ml/2–3tbsp each of orange liqueur and brandy in a small saucepan over a medium heat. Remove the pan from the heat, carefully ignite the liquid with a match then gently pour over the crêpes. Scatter over the orange segments and serve at once.

Mini Millefeuille

This pâtisserie *classic is a delectable combination of tender puff pastry sandwiched with luscious*

pastry cream. It is difficult to cut, making individual servings a brilliant solution.

INGREDIENTS

450g/1lb rough-puff or puff pastry
6 egg yolks
70g/2½oz/⅓ cup caster sugar
45ml/3 tbsp plain flour
350ml/12fl oz/1½ cups milk
30ml/2 tbsp Kirsch or cherry liqueur
(optional)
450g/1lb/2⅔ cups raspberries
icing sugar, for dusting
strawberry or raspberry coulis, to serve

Serves 8

1 Lightly butter two large baking sheets and then sprinkle them very lightly with cold water.

2 On a lightly floured surface, roll out the pastry to a 3mm/⅛in thickness. Using a 10cm/4in cutter, cut out 12 rounds. Place on the baking sheets and prick with a fork. Chill for 30 minutes. Preheat the oven to 200°C/400°F/Gas 6.

3 Bake the pastry rounds for about 15–20 minutes until golden, then transfer to wire racks to cool.

4 Whisk the egg yolks and sugar until light and creamy, then whisk in the flour until blended. Bring the milk to the boil and pour it over the egg mixture, whisking. Return to the saucepan, bring to the boil and boil for 2 minutes, whisking. Remove the pan from the heat and whisk in the Kirsch or liqueur. Pour into a bowl and press clear film on to the surface to prevent a skin forming. Set aside to cool.

5 To assemble, split the pastry rounds in half. Spread one round at a time with a little pastry cream. Arrange a layer of raspberries over the cream and top with a second pastry round. Spread with a little more cream and a few more raspberries. Top with a third pastry round flat side up. Dust with icing sugar and serve with the coulis.

RED FRUIT FILO BASKETS

This elegant dessert looks very festive. It is also low in fat and needs only a fine brushing of oil

before use: a light oil such as sunflower is the best choice for this recipe.

INGREDIENTS

3 sheets filo pastry (about 90g/3½oz)
15ml/1 tbsp sunflower oil
175g/6oz/1½ cups redcurrants
250ml/8fl oz/1 cup strained plain yogurt
5ml/1 tsp icing sugar
115 g/4 oz/1 cup whole strawberries and
raspberries, to decorate

Serves 6

1 Preheat the oven to 200°C/400°F/ Gas 6. Using a sharp kitchen knife, cut the sheets of filo pastry into 18 squares with sides about 10cm/4in long.

3 Reserve a few sprigs of redcurrants to add to the decoration and string the rest through the tines of a fork. Stir the currants into the yogurt.

4 Spoon the yogurt into the filo baskets. Decorate the baskets with the red fruits and sprinkle them lightly with icing sugar.

2 Brush each filo square thinly with oil, then arrange the squares to overlap in six small tartlet pans, layering them in threes. Bake for 6–8 minutes, until crisp and golden. Remove the baskets from the tartlet pans, using a palette knife, and allow them to cool.

CRUNCHY APPLE AND ALMOND FLAN

Do not be tempted to put any sugar with the apples, as this makes them produce too

much liquid. All the sweetness you'll need is in the pastry and topping.

INGREDIENTS

75g/3oz/6 tbsp butter
175g/6oz/1½ cups plain flour
25g/1oz/scant ⅓ cup ground almonds
25g/1oz/2 tbsp caster sugar
1 egg yolk
15ml/1 tbsp cold water
1.5ml/¼ tsp almond essence
sifted icing sugar, to decorate

For the Crunchy Topping
115g/4oz/1 cup plain flour
1.5ml/¼ tsp mixed spice
50g/2oz/4 tbsp butter, cut in small cubes
50g/2oz/4 tbsp demerara sugar
50g/2oz/½ cup flaked almonds

For the filling
675g/1½lb cooking apples
25g/1oz/2 tbsp raisins or sultanas

Serves 8

1 To make the pastry, rub the butter into the flour, either with your fingertips in a large mixing bowl or in a food processor, until it resembles fine breadcrumbs. Stir in the ground almonds and sugar. Whisk the egg yolk, water and almond essence together and mix them into the dry ingredients to form a soft, pliable dough. Knead the dough lightly until smooth, wrap in clear film and leave in a cool place or in the fridge to rest for about 20 minutes.

2 Meanwhile, make the crunchy topping. Sift the flour and mixed spice into a bowl and rub in the butter. Stir in the sugar and almonds.

3 Roll out the pastry on a lightly floured surface and use it to line a 23cm/9in loose-based flan tin, taking care to press it neatly into the edges and to make a lip around the top edge.

4 Roll off the excess pastry to neaten the edge. Allow to chill in the fridge for about 15 minutes.

5 Preheat the oven to 190°C/375°F/ Gas 5. Place a baking sheet in the oven to preheat. Peel, core and slice the apples thinly. Arrange the slices in the flan in overlapping, concentric circles, doming the centre. Scatter over the raisins or sultanas. The flan will seem too full at this stage, but as the apples cook the filling will drop slightly.

6 Cover the apples with the crunchy topping mixture, pressing it on lightly. Bake on the hot baking sheet for 25– 30 minutes, or until the top is golden brown and the apples are tender (test them with a fine skewer). Leave the flan to cool in the tin for 10 minutes before turning out. The flan can be served either warm or cool, dusted with sifted icing sugar.

Mango and Amaretti Strudel

Fresh mango and crushed amaretti wrapped in wafer-thin filo pastry make a

seasonal treat that is equally delicious made with apricots or plums.

INGREDIENTS

1 large mango
grated rind of 1 lemon
2 amaretti biscuits
25g/1oz/3 tbsp demerara sugar
60ml/4 tbsp wholemeal breadcrumbs
2 sheets of filo pastry, each
48 x 28cm/19 x 11in
20g/¾oz/4 tsp soft margarine, melted
15ml/1 tbsp chopped almonds
icing sugar, for dusting

Serves 4

1 Preheat the oven to 190°C/375°F/ Gas 5. Lightly grease a large baking sheet. Halve, stone and peel the mango. Cut the flesh into cubes, then place them in a bowl and sprinkle with the grated lemon rind.

2 Crush the amaretti biscuits with a rolling pin and mix them with the demerara sugar and the wholemeal breadcrumbs.

3 Lay one sheet of filo on a flat surface and brush with a quarter of the melted margarine. Top with the second sheet, brush with one-third of the remaining margarine, then fold both sheets over, if necessary, to make a rectangle measuring 28 x 24cm/11 x 9½in. Brush the rectangle with half the remaining margarine.

4 Sprinkle the filo with the amaretti mixture, leaving a 5cm/2in border on each long side. Arrange the mango cubes over the top.

5 Roll up the filo from one of the long sides, Swiss roll fashion. Lift the strudel on to the baking sheet with the join underneath. Brush with the remaining melted margarine and sprinkle with the chopped almonds.

6 Bake the strudel for 20–25 minutes until golden brown, then carefully transfer it to a board. Dust the strudel with the icing sugar, slice diagonally and serve warm.

COOK'S TIP

The easiest way to prepare a mango is to cut horizontally through the fruit, keeping the knife blade close to the stone. Repeat on the other side of the stone and peel off the skin. Remove the remaining skin and flesh from around the stone.

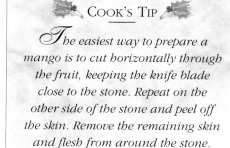

TRADITIONAL CHRISTMAS PUDDING

This recipe makes enough to fill one 1.2 litre/2 pint/5 cup basin or two 600ml/1 pint/2½ cup basins.

It can be made up to a month before Christmas and stored in a cool, dry place.

Steam the pudding for 2 hours before serving. Serve topped with a decorative sprig of holly.

INGREDIENTS

115g/4oz/½ cup butter
225g/8oz/1 heaped cup soft dark brown sugar
50g/2oz/½ cup self-raising flour
5ml/1 tsp mixed spice
1.5ml/¼ tsp nutmeg
2.5ml/½ tsp ground cinnamon
2 eggs
115g/4oz/2 cups fresh white breadcrumbs
175g/6oz/1 cup sultanas
175g/6oz/1 cup raisins
115g/4oz/½ cup currants
25g/1oz/3 tbsp chopped mixed peel
25g/1oz/¼ cup chopped almonds
1 small cooking apple, peeled, cored and coarsely grated
finely grated rind of 1 orange or lemon
juice of 1 orange or lemon, made up to 150ml/¼ pint/⅔ cup with brandy, rum or sherry

Serves 8

1 Cut a disc of greaseproof paper to fit the base of the basin(s) and butter the disc and basin(s).

2 Whisk the butter and sugar together until soft. Beat in the flour, spices and eggs. Stir in the remaining ingredients thoroughly. The mixture should have a soft dropping consistency.

3 Turn the mixture into the greased basin(s) and level the top.

4 Cover with another disc of buttered greaseproof paper.

5 Make a pleat across the centre of a large piece of greaseproof paper and cover the basin(s), tying it with string. Pleat a piece of foil in the same way and cover the basin(s), tucking it under the greaseproof frill.

6 Tie another piece of string around the basin(s) and across the top, as a handle. Place the basin(s) in a steamer over a pan of simmering water and steam for 6 hours. Alternatively, put the basin(s) into a large pan and pour round enough boiling water to come halfway up the basin(s) and cover the pan with a tight-fitting lid. Check the water is simmering and top it up with boiling water as it evaporates. When the pudding(s) have cooked, leave to cool completely. Then remove the foil and greaseproof paper. Wipe the basin(s) clean and replace the greaseproof paper and foil with clean pieces, ready for reheating.

TO SERVE

Steam for 2 hours. Turn on to a plate and leave to stand for 5 minutes before removing the pudding basin (the steam will rise to the top of the basin and help to loosen the pudding).

CHOCOLATE AND CHESTNUT YULE LOG

This chocolate log is traditionally served at Christmas. Make it the day before it is needed

or some time in advance and freeze it. It makes an excellent dessert for a party.

INGREDIENTS

25g/1oz/2 tbsp plain flour
30ml/2 tbsp cocoa powder
pinch of salt
3 large eggs, separated
large pinch of cream of tartar
115g/4oz/8 tbsp caster sugar
2–3 drops almond essence
sifted cocoa powder and holly sprigs,
to decorate

For the Filling
15ml/1 tbsp rum or brandy
5ml/1 tsp powdered gelatine
115g/4oz plain chocolate, broken into
squares
50g/2oz/4 tbsp caster sugar
250g/8oz can chestnut purée
225ml/½ pint/1¼ cups double cream

Serves 8

1 Preheat the oven to 180°C/350°F/ Gas 4. Grease and line a 23 x 33cm/ 9 x 13in Swiss roll tin and line the base with non-stick baking paper. Sift the flour, cocoa and salt together on to a piece of greaseproof paper.

2 Put the egg whites into a large clean bowl and whisk them until frothy. Add the cream of tartar and whisk until stiff. Gradually whisk in half the sugar, until the mixture will stand in stiff peaks.

3 Put the egg yolks and the remaining sugar into another bowl and whisk until thick and pale. Add the almond essence. Stir in the sifted flour and cocoa mixture. Lastly, fold in the egg whites, using a metal spoon, until everything is evenly blended. Be careful not to over-mix.

4 Turn the mixture into the prepared Swiss roll tin and level the top. Bake for 15–20 minutes, or until springy to the touch. Have ready a large piece of greaseproof paper dusted liberally with caster sugar. Turn the Swiss roll on to the paper, remove the baking lining paper, and roll it up with the greaseproof paper still inside. Leave to cool completely on a wire rack.

5 Put the rum or brandy in a cup and sprinkle over the gelatine; leave to become spongy. Melt the chocolate in a 600ml/1 pint/2½ cup basin over a pan of hot water. Melt the gelatine over barely simmering water and add to the chocolate. With an electric beater, whisk in the sugar and chestnut purée. Remove from the heat and leave to cool. Whisk the cream until it holds soft peaks. Fold the two mixtures together evenly.

6 Unroll the Swiss roll carefully, spread it with half the filling and roll it up again. Place it on a serving dish and spread over the rest of the chocolate cream to cover it. Mark it with a fork to resemble a log. Chill until firm. Dust the cake with sifted cocoa powder and decorate around the edges of the plate with sprigs of holly.

Frozen Grand Marnier Soufflés

These luxurious puddings are always appreciated and make a wonderful end to any Christmas-time meal.

INGREDIENTS

200g/7oz/1 cup caster sugar
6 large eggs, separated
250ml/8fl oz/1 cup milk
15g/½oz powdered gelatine, soaked in
45ml/3 tbsp cold water
450ml/¾ pint/1⅞ cups double cream
60ml/4 tbsp Grand Marnier

Serves 8

1 Fold a double collar of greaseproof paper around eight ramekin dishes and tie with string. (You could make one large pudding, if you prefer.) Put 75g/3oz/6 tbsp of the caster sugar in a large mixing bowl with the egg yolks and whisk until the yolks are pale. This will take about 5 minutes by hand and about 3 minutes if you use an electric hand mixer.

2 Heat the milk until almost boiling and pour it on to the yolks, whisking all the time. Return to the pan and stir it over a gentle heat until it is thick enough to coat the back of the spoon. Remove the pan from the heat. Stir the soaked gelatine into the custard. Pour into a bowl and leave to cool. Whisk occasionally, until the custard is on the point of setting.

3 Put the remaining sugar in a pan with the water and dissolve it over a low heat. Bring to the boil and boil rapidly until it reaches the soft ball stage or 119°C/238°F on a sugar thermometer. Remove from the heat. In a clean bowl, whisk the egg whites until they are stiff. Pour the hot syrup on to the whites, whisking all the time. Leave to cool.

4 Whisk the cream until it holds soft peaks. Add the Grand Marnier to the cold custard and fold into the cold meringue, with the cream. Pour into the prepared ramekin dishes. Freeze overnight. Remove the paper collars. Leave at room temperature for 30 minutes before serving.

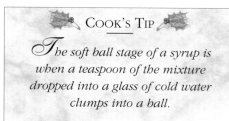

COOK'S TIP

The soft ball stage of a syrup is when a teaspoon of the mixture dropped into a glass of cold water clumps into a ball.

Tiramisu in Chocolate Cups

Give in to the temptation of tiramisu, with its magical mocha flavour.

Ingredients

1 egg yolk
30ml/2 tbsp caster sugar
2.5ml/½ tsp vanilla essence
250g/9oz/generous cup mascarpone cheese
120ml/4fl oz/½ cup strong black coffee
15ml/1 tbsp cocoa powder
30ml/2 tbsp coffee liqueur
16 amaretti biscuits
cocoa powder, for dusting

For the Chocolate Cups
175g/6oz good quality plain chocolate, broken into squares
25g/1oz/2 tbsp unsalted butter

Serves 6

Cook's Tip

When spreading the chocolate for the cups, don't aim for perfectly regular edges; uneven edges will give a prettier frilled effect.

1 Make the chocolate cups. Cut out six 15cm/6in rounds of non-stick baking paper. Melt the chocolate with the butter in a heatproof bowl over barely simmering water. Stir until smooth, then spread a spoonful of the chocolate mixture over each circle, to within 2cm/¾in of the edge.

2 Carefully lift each paper round and drape it over an upturned teacup or ramekin so that the edges curve into frills. Leave until completely set, then carefully lift off and peel away the paper to reveal the chocolate cups.

3 To make the filling, beat the egg yolk and sugar in a bowl until smooth, then stir in the vanilla essence and mascarpone. Mix until a smooth, creamy consistency is achieved.

4 In a separate bowl, mix the coffee, cocoa and liqueur. Break up the biscuits and stir into the mixture.

5 Divide half the biscuit mixture among the chocolate cups, then spoon over half the mascarpone mixture.

6 Spoon over the remaining biscuit mixture, top with the rest of the mascarpone mixture and dust with cocoa. Serve as soon as possible.

Iced Praline Torte

Make this elaborate torte several days ahead, decorate it and return it to the freezer until you

are nearly ready to serve it. Allow the torte to stand at room temperature for an hour before

serving, or leave it in the refrigerator overnight to soften.

INGREDIENTS

115g/4oz/1 cup almonds or hazelnuts
115g/4oz/8 tbsp caster sugar
115g/4oz/²⁄₃ cup raisins
90ml/6 tbsp rum or brandy
115g/4oz plain chocolate, broken into
squares
30ml/2 tbsp milk
450ml/³⁄₄ pint/1⅞ cups double cream
30ml/2 tbsp strong black coffee
16 sponge-finger biscuits

To Finish

150ml/¼ pint/²⁄₃ cup double cream
50g/2oz/½ cup flaked almonds, toasted
15g/½oz plain chocolate, melted

Serves 8

1 To make the praline, have ready an oiled cake tin or baking sheet. Put the nuts into a heavy-based saucepan with the sugar and heat gently until the sugar melts. Swirl the pan to coat the nuts in the hot sugar. Cook slowly until the nuts brown and the sugar caramelizes. Watch all the time, as this will only take a few minutes. Turn the nuts quickly into the cake tin or on to the baking sheet and leave them to cool completely. When cool, break the praline up and grind it to a fine powder in a food processor.

2 Soak the raisins in 45ml/3 tbsp of the rum or brandy for an hour (or better still overnight), so they soften and absorb the full flavour of the alcohol. Melt the chocolate with the milk in a bowl over a pan of barely simmering water. Remove and allow to cool. Lightly grease a 1.2 litre/ 2 pint/5 cup loaf tin and line it with greaseproof paper.

3 Whisk the cream in a bowl until it holds soft peaks. Whisk in the cold chocolate. Then fold in the praline and the soaked raisins, with any liquid.

4 Mix the coffee and remaining rum or brandy in a shallow dish. Dip in each of the sponge-finger biscuits and arrange half in a layer over the base of the prepared loaf tin.

5 Cover the sponge biscuits with the chocolate mixture and add another layer of soaked sponge fingers. Freeze overnight.

6 Dip the cake tin briefly into warm water to loosen it and turn the torte out on to a serving plate. Cover with whipped cream. Sprinkle the top with toasted flaked almonds and drizzle the melted chocolate over the top. Return the torte to the freezer until it is needed.

COOK'S TIP

Praline is a delicious crunchy caramel and nut mixture. It doesn't matter whether you use hazelnuts or almonds – or even a mixture of the two, if you prefer.

BAKED CUSTARD WITH BURNT SUGAR

You can add a little liqueur to this dessert if you like, but it is equally delicious without it.

INGREDIENTS

2 vanilla pods
1 litre/1¾ pints/4 cups double cream
6 egg yolks
100g/3½oz/½ cup caster sugar
30ml/2 tbsp almond or orange liqueur
75g/3oz/⅓ cup soft light brown sugar

Serves 6

1 Preheat the oven to 150°C/300°F/ Gas 2. Place six 120ml/4fl oz/½ cup ramekins in a roasting tin or ovenproof dish and set aside.

2 With a sharp knife, split the vanilla pods lengthways. Scrape the black seeds into a medium saucepan and add the pods. Add the cream and bring just to the boil over a medium-high heat, stirring frequently. Remove from the heat and cover. Set aside to stand for 15–20 minutes. This will allow the vanilla to infuse the cream.

3 In a bowl, whisk the egg yolks, caster sugar and liqueur until well blended. Whisk in the hot cream and strain into a large jug. Divide the custard equally among the ramekins.

4 Pour enough boiling water into the roasting tin to come halfway up the sides of the ramekins. Cover the tin with foil and bake in the preheated oven for about 30 minutes until the custards are just set. Remove the ramekins from the tin and leave to cool. Return to the dry roasting tin and allow to chill in the fridge for at least 2 hours or overnight.

5 Preheat the grill. Sprinkle the sugar evenly over the surface of each custard and grill for 30–60 seconds until the sugar melts and caramelizes. (Do not let the sugar burn or the custard curdle.) Place in the fridge again to set the crust and chill completely before serving.

CHRISTMAS CRANBERRY BOMBE

This is a light alternative to Christmas pudding that is still very festive.

INGREDIENTS

For the Sorbet Centre
*225g/8oz/2 cups fresh or frozen
cranberries
150ml/¼ pint/⅔ cup orange juice
finely grated rind of ½ orange
2.5ml/½ tsp allspice
60ml/4 tbsp raw sugar*

For the Outer Layer
*600ml/1 pint/2⅔ cups vanilla ice cream
30ml/2 tbsp chopped angelica
30ml/2 tbsp candied citrus rind
15ml/1 tbsp slivered almonds, toasted*

Serves 6

3 Pack the mixture into a 5 cup pudding mould and, using a metal spoon, hollow out the centre. Freeze the mould until firm to the touch. This will take at least 3 hours.

4 Fill the hollowed-out centre of the bombe with cranberry mixture, smooth over and freeze until firm. To serve, allow to soften slightly at room temperature, turn out and slice.

1 Put the cranberries, orange juice, rind and spice in a pan and cook gently until the cranberries are soft. Add the sugar, then purée in a food processor until almost smooth, but still with some texture. Leave to cool.

2 Allow the vanilla ice cream to soften slightly then stir in the chopped angelica, mixed peel and almonds.

CHOCOLATE SORBET WITH RED FRUITS

This velvety smooth sorbet has long been a favourite. Bitter chocolate gives by far the richest flavour, but if you can't track this down, then use 250g/9oz of the very best quality dark Continental plain chocolate that you can find. If not the sorbet will be too sweet.

INGREDIENTS

150g/5oz bitter chocolate, roughly chopped
115g/4oz plain chocolate, roughly chopped
200g/7oz/1 cup caster sugar
475ml/16fl oz/2 cups water
chocolate curls, to decorate
sprigs of fresh berries, to decorate

Serves 6

1 Put the chopped bitter and plain chocolate in a food processor fitted with a metal blade, and process for 20–30 seconds until the chunks of chocolate are finely chopped.

2 In a large heavy-based saucepan over a medium-high heat, bring the sugar and water to the boil, stirring continuously, until the sugar dissolves. Boil for about 2 minutes, then remove the saucepan from the heat.

3 With the food processor running, pour the hot syrup over the chocolate. Allow the machine to continue running for 1–2 minutes until the chocolate is completely melted and the mixture is smooth, scraping down the bowl once.

4 Strain the chocolate mixture into a large measuring jug or bowl, and leave to cool, then chill, stirring occasionally. Freeze the mixture in an ice cream machine, following the manufacturer's instructions or see Cook's Tip (below). Allow the sorbet to soften for 5–10 minutes at room temperature and serve in scoops, decorated with chocolate curls and the sprigs of fresh berries.

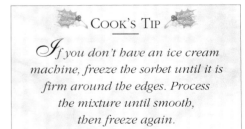

COOK'S TIP

If you don't have an ice cream machine, freeze the sorbet until it is firm around the edges. Process the mixture until smooth, then freeze again.

Amaretto Mousses with Chocolate Sauce

These little desserts are extremely rich and derive their flavour from Amaretto, an

almond-flavoured liqueur, and amaretti, little almond-flavoured biscuits.

Ingredients

*115g/4oz amaretti, ratafia or macaroon
biscuits
60ml/4 tbsp Amaretto di Sarono liqueur
350g/12oz white chocolate, broken into
squares
15g/½oz powdered gelatine, soaked in
45ml/3 tbsp cold water
450ml/¾ pint/1⅞ cups double cream*

*For the Chocolate Sauce
225g/8oz dark chocolate, broken into
squares
300ml/½ pint/1¼ cups single cream
50g/2oz/4 tbsp caster sugar*

Serves 8

1 Lightly oil eight individual 120ml/
4fl oz/½ cup moulds and line the base
of each mould with a small disc of
oiled greaseproof paper. Put the
biscuits into a large bowl and crush
them finely with a rolling pin.

2 Melt the Amaretto and white
chocolate together gently in a bowl
over a pan of hot but not boiling
water (be very careful not to overheat
the chocolate or it will begin to
separate and go unpleasantly grainy).
Stir well until smooth; remove from
the pan and leave to cool.

3 Melt the gelatine over hot water
and blend it into the chocolate
mixture. Whisk the cream until it
holds soft peaks. Gently fold in the
chocolate mixture, with 60ml/4 tbsp
of the crushed biscuits.

4 Put a teaspoonful of the crushed
biscuits into the bottom of each mould
and spoon in the chocolate mixture.
Tap each mould to disperse any air
bubbles. Level the tops and sprinkle
the remaining crushed biscuits on top.
Press down gently and chill for 4 hours.

5 To make the chocolate sauce, put
all the ingredients in a small saucepan
and heat gently to melt the chocolate
and dissolve the sugar. Simmer for
2–3 minutes. Leave to cool completely.

6 Slip a knife around the sides of each
mould, and turn out on to individual
plates. Remove the greaseproof paper
from the bottom and pour round a little
dark chocolate sauce.

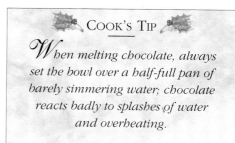

Cook's Tip

*When melting chocolate, always
set the bowl over a half-full pan of
barely simmering water; chocolate
reacts badly to splashes of water
and overheating.*

CHOCOLATE CRÊPES WITH PLUMS AND PORT

A good dinner party dessert, this dish can be made in advance and always looks impressive.

INGREDIENTS

*50g/2oz plain chocolate, broken into
squares
200ml/7fl oz/scant 1 cup milk
120ml/4fl oz/½ cup single cream
30ml/2 tbsp cocoa powder
115g/4oz/1 cup plain flour
2 eggs
oil, for frying*

For the Filling
*500g/1¼ lb red or golden plums
50g/2oz/¼ cup caster sugar
30ml/2 tbsp water
30ml/2 tbsp port
175g/6oz/¾ cup crème fraîche*

For the Sauce
*150g/5oz plain chocolate, broken into
squares
175ml/6fl oz/¾ cup double cream
30ml/2 tbsp port*

Serves 6

1 Place the chocolate in a saucepan with the milk. Heat gently until the chocolate has dissolved. Pour into a blender or food processor and add the cream, cocoa powder, flour and eggs. Process until smooth, then tip into a jug and chill for 30 minutes.

2 Meanwhile, make the filling. Halve and stone the plums. Place them in a saucepan and add the sugar and water. Bring to the boil, then cover and simmer for about 10 minutes. Stir in the port; simmer for a further 30 seconds. Remove from the heat and keep warm.

3 Have ready a sheet of non-stick baking paper. Heat a crêpe pan, grease it lightly with a little oil, then pour in just enough batter to cover the base of the pan, swirling to coat evenly. Cook until the crêpe has set, then flip it over to cook the other side. Slide the crêpe out on to the sheet of paper, then cook 9–11 more crêpes in the same way.

4 Make the chocolate sauce. Combine the chocolate and cream in a saucepan. Heat gently, stirring until smooth. Add the port and heat gently for 1 minute.

5 Divide the plum filling between the crêpes, add a generous spoonful of crème fraîche to each and roll them up. Serve with the chocolate sauce.

CHOCOLATE, DATE AND ALMOND FILO COIL

Experience the allure of the Middle East with this delectable dessert. Crisp filo pastry conceals

a chocolate and rose water filling studded with dates and almonds.

INGREDIENTS

275g/10oz packet filo pastry, thawed if frozen
50g/2oz/4 tbsp unsalted butter, melted
icing sugar, cocoa powder and ground cinnamon, for dusting

For the Filling
75g/3oz/6 tbsp unsalted butter
115g/4oz plain chocolate, broken into squares
115g/4oz/1 cup ground almonds
115g/4oz/⅔ cup chopped dates
75g/3oz/⅔ cup icing sugar
10ml/2 tsp rose water
2.5ml/½ tsp ground cinnamon

Serves 6

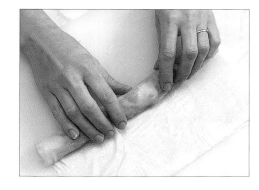

3 Roll a handful of the chocolate almond mixture into a long sausage shape and place along one edge of the filo. Roll the pastry tightly around.

4 Place the roll around the outside of the tin. Make enough rolls to fill the tin.

5 Brush the coil with the remaining melted butter. Bake for 30–35 minutes until the pastry is golden brown and crisp. Remove the coil from the tin; place it on a plate. Serve warm, dusted with icing sugar, cocoa and cinnamon.

1 Preheat the oven to 180°C/350°F/ Gas 4. Grease a 22cm/8½in round cake tin. Make the chocolate, date and almond filling. Melt the butter with the chocolate in a heatproof bowl over a saucepan of barely simmering water, then remove the saucepan from the heat and stir in all of the remaining ingredients to make a thick paste. Set the pan aside to cool.

2 Lay one sheet of the filo pastry on a clean work surface. Brush the filo with melted butter, then lay a second sheet of filo on top and brush again with butter.

RASPBERRY AND WHITE CHOCOLATE CHEESECAKE

Raspberries and white chocolate are an irresistible combination, especially when

teamed with smooth, rich mascarpone cheese on a crunchy ginger and pecan nut base.

INGREDIENTS

50g/2oz/4 tbsp unsalted butter
225g/8oz ginger nut biscuits, crushed
50g/2oz/½ cup chopped pecan nuts or walnuts

For the Filling
275g/10oz/1¼ cups mascarpone cheese
175g/6oz/¾ cup fromage frais
2 eggs, beaten
45ml/3 tbsp caster sugar
250g/9oz white chocolate, broken into squares
225g/8oz/1½ cups fresh or frozen raspberries

For the Topping
115g/4 oz/½ cup mascarpone cheese
75g/3oz/⅓ cup fromage frais
white chocolate curls and raspberries, to decorate

Serves 8

2 To make the filling, beat the mascarpone cheese and fromage frais in a bowl, then beat in the eggs and caster sugar until evenly mixed.

3 Melt the white chocolate gently in a heatproof bowl over hot water, then stir into the cheese mixture with the fresh or frozen raspberries.

4 Tip into the prepared tin and spread evenly, then bake for about 1 hour or until just set. Switch off the oven, but do not remove the cheesecake. Leave it until cold and completely set.

5 Remove the sides of the tin and carefully lift the cheesecake on to a serving plate. Make the topping by mixing together the mascarpone and fromage frais in a bowl and spreading the mixture over the cheesecake. Decorate with white chocolate curls and the fresh raspberries.

COOK'S TIP

The biscuits for the base should be crushed quite finely. This can easily be done in a food processor. Alternatively, place the biscuits in a stout plastic bag and crush them with a rolling pin.

1 Preheat the oven to 150°C/300°F/Gas 2. Melt the butter in a large saucepan, then stir in the crushed biscuits and nuts. Press the mixture into the base of a 23cm/9in springform cake tin.

CHOCOLATE ROULADE WITH COCONUT CREAM

This sinfully rich roulade is the ultimate in Christmas treats.

It makes the perfect dessert for a New Year's Eve dinner party.

INGREDIENTS

150g/5oz/³⁄₄ cup caster sugar
5 eggs, separated
50g/2oz/¹⁄₂ cup cocoa powder

For the Filling
300ml/¹⁄₂ pint/1¹⁄₄ cups double cream
45ml/3 tbsp whisky
50g/2oz piece solid creamed coconut
30ml/2 tbsp caster sugar

For the Topping
coarsely grated curls of fresh coconut
chocolate curls

Serves 8

1 Preheat the oven to 180°C/350°F/ Gas 4. Grease a 33 x 23cm/13 x 9in Swiss roll tin. Dust a large sheet of greaseproof paper with 30ml/2 tbsp of caster sugar.

2 Place the egg yolks in a heatproof bowl. Add the remaining caster sugar and whisk with a hand-held electric mixer until the mixture is thick enough to leave a trail. Sift the cocoa over, then fold in carefully and evenly with a metal spoon.

3 Whisk the egg whites in a clean, grease-free bowl until they form soft peaks. Fold about 15ml/1 tbsp of the whites into the chocolate mixture to lighten it, then fold in the rest evenly.

4 Scrape the mixture into the prepared tin, taking it right into the corners. Smooth the surface with a palette knife, then bake for 20–25 minutes or until well risen and springy to the touch.

5 Turn the cooked sponge out on to the sugar-dusted greaseproof paper and carefully peel off the lining paper. Cover with a damp, clean dish towel and leave to cool.

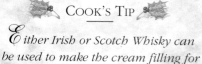

COOK'S TIP

Either Irish or Scotch Whisky can be used to make the cream filling for this dessert. If whisky is not available, you can use white rum or a rum-based spirit, such as Malibu, as a suitable alternative.

6 To make the filling, whisk the cream with the whisky in a bowl until the mixture just holds its shape, then finely grate the creamed coconut and stir it in with the sugar.

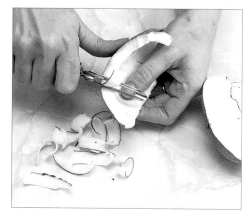

7 Remove the dish towel to uncover the sponge. Spread about three-quarters of the cream mixture to the edges of the sponge. Roll up carefully from a long side. Transfer the roulade to a plate and pipe or spoon the remaining cream mixture on top. Then grate the fresh coconut to make the curls and place them on top, along with the chocolate curls.

Christmas Baking

*N*uts and spices, dried fruit and mincemeat all
mean Christmas and the delicious cakes and biscuits baked
during this time. Some, like the Moist and Rich Christmas
Cake, need advance preparation, while others, like the
Christmas Biscuits, are simple enough to make with the
children. Gingerbread is essential to Christmas and there are
recipes here to double as pretty tree decorations and a table
centrepiece. There is the traditional Italian Panettone and
Austrian Stollen, Hogmanay Shortbread and Middle Eastern
Date-filled Pastries. Finally, there are three lovely recipes
with mincemeat – the all-time favourite – to ensure that
everyone finishes the festive meal feeling satisfied.

FESTIVE GINGERBREAD

In all its forms, gingerbread has been part of the Christmas tradition for generations.

It is particularly well-loved in Germany, from where many present-day baking traditions originate.

INGREDIENTS

30ml/2 tbsp golden syrup
15ml/1 tbsp black treacle
50g/2oz/¼ cup soft light brown sugar
25g/1oz/2 tbsp butter
175g/6oz/1½ cups plain flour
3.5ml/¾ tsp bicarbonate of soda
2.5ml/½ tsp mixed spice
7.5ml/1½ tsp ground ginger
1 egg yolk

Icing and Decoration
½ quantity royal icing (see Introduction)
red, yellow and green food colourings
brightly coloured ribbons

Makes 20

1 Preheat the oven to 190°C/375°F/ Gas 5. Line several baking sheets with non-stick baking paper. Place the syrup, treacle, sugar and butter in a saucepan. Heat gently, stirring occasionally, until the butter has melted into the syrup.

2 Sift the flour, bicarbonate of soda, mixed spice and ginger together in a mixing bowl. Using a wooden spoon, stir in the treacle mixture and the egg yolk and mix to form a soft dough. Remove the dough from the bowl and knead on a lightly floured surface until smooth.

3 Roll out the dough thinly, and using a selection of festive cutters such as stars and Christmas trees, stamp out as many shapes as possible, kneading and re-rolling the dough as necessary. Arrange the shapes, well spaced apart, on the baking sheets. Make a hole in the top of each shape, using a drinking straw, if you wish to use the biscuits as hanging decorations.

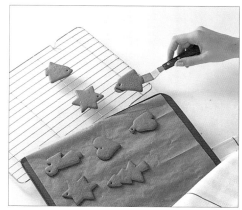

4 Bake in the oven for 15–20 minutes or until risen and golden and leave to cool on the baking sheets before transferring to a wire rack using a palette knife.

5 Divide the royal icing into 4 and colour ¼ red, ¼ yellow and ¼ green using the food colourings. Make 4 greaseproof paper piping bags and fill each one with the different coloured icings. Fold down the tops and snip off the points.

6 Pipe lines, dots, and zigzags on the gingerbread biscuits using the coloured icings. Leave to dry. If you intend to hang the biscuits, thread ribbons through the holes made in the biscuits.

COOK'S TIP

These brightly decorated gingerbread biscuits are fun to make and may be used as edible Christmas tree decorations.

GINGERBREAD HEART RING

This table centrepiece is inspired by traditional Polish Christmas decorations. You could make the

centrepiece with other cut-out shapes, such as gingerbread men and women, teddy bears or stars.

EQUIPMENT

stiff cardboard
pencil and scissors
glacé icing made with 115g/4oz/1 cup
sifted icing sugar and, if you wish,
coloured red
palette knife
7 heart-shaped gingerbread biscuits,
baked and decorated
5cm/2in-wide ribbon
Victorian-style paper scraps (optional)

1 On a piece of stiff cardboard, draw a ring shape with an outer diameter of 25cm/10in and an inner diameter of 15cm/6in. Cut out the ring with a pair of scissors. Cover the cardboard ring with the glacé icing, using a palette knife, and quickly – before it sets – press on the heart-shaped gingerbread biscuits to cover it. Set the ring aside until the glacé icing has dried and the gingerbread biscuits are fixed in place.

2 Tie the ribbon into a bow, trim the ends and fix it to the ring with a generous dab of glacé icing to ensure it stays securely in place throughout the season. To preserve the ring as a decoration throughout the Christmas holidays, it may be as well to make extra heart-shaped biscuits for young gingerbread enthusiasts to eat!

COOK'S TIP

Victorian scraps or other paper decorations can be fixed to the centre of each biscuit with a dab of glacé icing.

GLACÉ ICING

To make glacé icing, sift the required amount of icing sugar into a bowl. Add a few drops of water at a time, and beat into the icing sugar. Keep adding water, a little at a time, until the desired consistency has been achieved.

Nut and Glacé Fruit Ring

The cake can be made two or three weeks before Christmas. Store it in a tin in a cool place until needed.

INGREDIENTS

60ml/4 tbsp rum, brandy or sherry
115g/4oz/½ cup glacé cherries, quartered
115g/4oz/⅔ cup raisins or sultanas
115g/4oz dried apricots, quartered
115g/4oz/1 cup prunes, stoned and quartered
115g/4oz/½ cup stoned and chopped dates
115g/4oz/½ cup butter
115g/4oz/½ cup soft dark brown sugar
2.5ml/½ tsp ground cinnamon
2.5ml/½ tsp mixed spice
2 eggs, beaten
50g/2oz/⅔ cup ground almonds
115g/4oz/1 cup coarsely chopped walnuts
225g/8oz/2 cups self-raising flour

To Finish

30ml/2 tbsp rum, brandy or sherry
60ml/4 tbsp apricot jam
whole blanched almonds, split
3 glacé cherries, halved
few strips angelica

Makes 1 ring

3 Spoon the mixture into the prepared cake tin. Level the top of the mixture with the back of a spoon and bake in the preheated oven for 1½–2 hours. Leave the cake to cool in the tin for 30 minutes, then turn out on to a wire rack and allow to cool completely. Brush the cake with the rum, brandy or sherry.

4 Put the apricot jam in a small pan and heat it gently to melt it. Sieve the jam. Brush the hot glaze over the top of the cake. Arrange the nuts and fruit in a flower design on top of the cake and brush them liberally with more apricot glaze. The glaze must be used very hot, or the decoration will lift while you are brushing the jam over it.

1 The day before you want to bake the cake, put the rum, brandy or sherry in a large mixing bowl and add all the dried fruit. Cover the bowl with clear film and leave overnight in a cool place so that the fruit is well soaked. Meanwhile, grease a 23cm/ 9in ring mould, with a 1.5 litre/ 2½ pint/6¼ cup capacity.

2 The next day, preheat the oven to 160°C/325°F/Gas 3. In a large mixing bowl, whisk the butter, sugar and spices together until they are light and fluffy. Whisk in the eggs, and then fold in the soaked fruits, with any of the remaining liquid. Mix the ground almonds and chopped walnuts into the bowl and sift in the flour.

PANETTONE

This popular Italian cake is perfect for the festive season.

INGREDIENTS

150ml/¼ pint/⅔ cup lukewarm milk
1 packet easy-blend dried yeast
400g/12–14oz/3–3½ cups flour
60g/2½oz/¼ cup sugar
10ml/2 tsp salt
2 eggs
5 egg yolks
175g/6oz/¾ cup unsalted butter, at
room temperature
115g/4oz/¾ cup raisins
grated rind of 1 lemon
75g/3oz/½ cup candied citrus peel,
chopped

Makes 1 loaf

1 Combine the milk and yeast in a large, warmed mixing bowl and leave for 10 minutes to dissolve the yeast.

2 Sift in 115g/4oz/1 cup of the flour, stir in and cover loosely, and leave in a warm place for 30 minutes.

3 Sift over the remaining flour. Make a well in the centre and add the sugar, salt, eggs and egg yolks.

4 Stir the dough mixture with a wooden spoon until it becomes too stiff, then continue to stir the mixture with your hands to obtain a very elastic and sticky dough. Add a little more of the flour, if necessary, blending it in well, to keep the dough as soft as possible.

5 Smear the butter into the dough, then work it in with your hands. When evenly distributed, cover and leave to rise in a warm place until doubled in volume, 3–4 hours.

6 Line the bottom of a 2 litre/3½ pint/8 cup charlotte mould or 2 pound coffee can with greaseproof paper, then grease the bottom and sides.

7 Punch down the dough and transfer to a floured surface. Knead in the raisins, lemon rind, and citrus peel.

8 Transfer the dough to the mould. Cover with a plastic bag and leave to rise until the dough is well above the top of the container, about 2 hours.

9 Preheat the oven to 200°C/400°F/Gas 6. Bake for 15 minutes, cover with foil, and lower the heat to180°C/350°F/Gas 4. Bake for 30 minutes. Cool in the mould then transfer the cake to a rack.

STOLLEN

Stollen is a fruity yeast bread traditionally served in Austria and Germany at

Christmas-time. It may be served at breakfast with coffee or tea.

INGREDIENTS

150ml/¼ pint/⅔ cup lukewarm milk
40g/1½oz/3 tbsp caster sugar
10ml/2 tsp easy-blend dried yeast
350g/12oz/3 cups plain flour, plus extra for dusting
1.5ml/¼ tsp salt
100g/4oz/½ cup butter, softened
1 egg, beaten
50g/2oz/⅓ cup seedless raisins
25g/1oz/⅛ cup sultanas
40g/1½oz/¼ cup candied orange peel, chopped
25g/1oz/¼ cup blanched almonds, chopped
5ml/1 tbsp rum
40g/1½oz/3 tbsp butter, melted
about 50g/2oz/½ cup icing sugar

Makes 1 loaf

1 Mix together the warm milk, sugar and yeast and leave it in a warm place until it is frothy.

2 Sift together the flour and salt, make a well in the centre and pour on the yeast mixture. Add the softened butter and egg and mix to form a soft dough. Mix in the raisins, sultanas, peel and almonds and sprinkle on the rum. Knead the dough on a lightly floured board until it is pliable.

3 Place the dough in a large, greased mixing bowl, cover it with non-stick baking paper and set it aside in a warm place for about 2 hours, until it has doubled in size.

4 Turn the dough out on to a floured board and knead it lightly until it is smooth and elastic again. Shape the dough to a rectangle about 25 x 20cm/ 10 x 8in. Fold the dough over along one of the long sides and press the 2 layers together. Cover the loaf and leave it to stand for 20 minutes.

5 Heat the oven to 200°C/400°F/Gas 6. Bake the loaf in the oven for 25–30 minutes, until it is well risen. Allow it to cool slightly on the baking sheet, then brush it with melted butter. Sift the sugar over the top and transfer the loaf to a wire rack to cool. Serve the stollen in thin slices.

Light Jewelled Fruit Cake

This cake can be made up to two weeks before eating it. For serving, brush the top

with hot apricot jam and tie a pretty ribbon around the sides.

INGREDIENTS

115g/4oz/½ cup currants
115g/4oz/⅔ cup sultanas
225g/8oz/1 cup quartered glacé cherries
50g/2oz/½ cup finely chopped mixed candied peel
30ml/2 tbsp rum, brandy or sherry
225g/8oz/1 cup butter
225g/8oz/1 cup caster sugar
finely grated rind of 1 orange
finely grated rind of 1 lemon
4 eggs
50g/2oz/½ cup chopped almonds
50g/2oz/⅔ cup ground almonds
225g/8oz/2 cups plain flour

To Finish
50g/2oz whole blanched almonds

Makes 1 cake

1 The day before you want to bake the cake, soak the currants, sultanas, glacé cherries and the mixed peel in the rum, brandy or sherry. Cover with clear film and leave overnight. The day you bake the cake, grease and line a 20cm/8in round cake tin or an 18cm/7in square cake tin with a double thickness of greaseproof paper.

2 Preheat the oven to 160°C/325°F/Gas 3. In a large bowl, whisk the butter, sugar and orange and lemon rinds together until they are light and fluffy. Beat in the eggs, one at a time.

3 Mix in the chopped almonds, ground almonds, soaked fruits (with their liquid) and the flour, to make a soft dropping consistency. Spoon into the cake tin. Bake for 30 minutes.

4 Gently place the whole almonds in a pattern on top of the cake. Do not press them into the cake or they will sink during cooking. Return the cake to the oven and cook for a further 1½–2 hours, or until the centre is firm to the touch. Let the cake cool in the tin for 30 minutes. Then remove it and cool completely on a wire rack, but leave the paper on; this helps to keep the cake moist while stored.

Spiced Christmas Cake

This light cake mixture is flavoured with spices and fruit. It can be served with

a dusting of icing sugar and decorated with holly leaves.

INGREDIENTS

225g/8oz/1 cup butter, plus extra for greasing
15g/½oz/1 tbsp fresh white breadcrumbs
225g/8oz/1 cup caster sugar
50ml/2fl oz/¼ cup water
3 eggs, separated
225g/8oz/2 cups self-raising flour
7.5g/1½ tsp mixed spice
25g/1oz/2 tbsp chopped angelica
25g/1oz/2 tbsp mixed peel
50g/2oz/¼ cup chopped glacé cherries
50g/2oz/½ cup chopped walnuts
icing sugar, to dust

Makes 1 cake

2 Place the butter, sugar and water into a saucepan. Heat gently, stirring occasionally, until melted. Boil for 3 minutes until syrupy, then allow to cool. Place the egg whites in a clean bowl, whisk until stiff. Sift the flour and spice into a bowl, add the angelica, mixed peel, cherries and walnuts and stir well to mix. Add the egg yolks.

3 Pour the cooled mixture into the bowl and beat to form a soft batter. Gradually fold in the egg whites, until the mixture is evenly blended. Pour into the prepared mould and bake for 50–60 minutes or until the cake springs back when pressed in the centre. Turn out and allow to cool on a wire rack. Dust with icing sugar to serve.

1 Preheat the oven to 180˚C/350˚F/ Gas 4. Brush a 20cm/8in x 1.5 litre/ 2½ pint fluted ring mould with melted butter and coat with breadcrumbs, shaking out any excess.

Moist and Rich Christmas Cake

The cake can be made 4–6 weeks before Christmas. During this time, pierce the cake with a

fine needle and spoon over 30–45ml/2–3 tbsp brandy.

INGREDIENTS

225g/8oz/1⅓ cups sultanas
225g/8oz/1 cup currants
225g/8oz/1⅓ cups raisins
115g/4oz/1 cup stoned and chopped prunes
50g/2oz/¼ cup halved glacé cherries
50g/2oz/⅓ cup chopped mixed peel
45ml/3 tbsp brandy or sherry
225g/8oz/2 cups plain flour
pinch of salt
2.5ml/½ tsp ground cinnamon
2.5ml/½ tsp grated nutmeg
15ml/1 tbsp cocoa powder
225g/8oz/1 cup butter
225g/8oz/1 generous cup soft dark brown sugar
4 large eggs
finely grated rind of 1 orange or lemon
50g/2oz/⅔ cup ground almonds
50g/2oz/½ cup chopped almonds

To Decorate
(see Introduction)
60ml/4 tbsp apricot jam
450g/1lb almond paste
450g/1lb fondant icing
225g/8oz royal icing

Makes 1 cake

1 The day before you want to bake the cake, soak the dried fruit in the brandy or sherry, cover and leave overnight. The next day, grease a 20cm/8in round cake tin and line it with greaseproof paper.

2 Preheat the oven to 160°C/325°F/Gas 3. Sift together the flour, salt, spices and cocoa powder. Whisk the butter and sugar together until light and fluffy and beat in the eggs gradually. Finally, mix in the orange or lemon rind, the ground and chopped almonds, dried fruits (with any liquid) and the flour mixture.

3 Spoon into the cake tin, level the top and give the cake tin a gentle tap on the work surface to disperse any air bubbles. Bake for 3 hours, or until a fine skewer inserted into the middle comes out clean. Transfer the cake tin to a wire rack and let the cake cool in the tin for an hour. Then turn the cake out on to the wire rack, but leave the paper on, as it will help to keep the cake moist during storage. When the cake is cold, wrap it in foil and store it in a cool place.

4 Warm, then sieve the apricot jam to make a glaze. Remove the paper from the cake, place it in the centre of the cake board and brush it with hot apricot glaze. Cover the cake with a layer of almond paste and then a layer of fondant icing. Pipe a border around the base of the cake with royal cing. Tie a ribbon around the sides.

5 Roll out any trimmings from the fondant icing and stamp out 12 small holly leaves with a cutter. Make one bell motif with a biscuit mould, dusted first with sifted icing sugar. Roll 36 small balls for the holly berries. Leave the decorations on greaseproof paper to dry for 24 hours. Decorate the cake with the fondant icing leaves, berries and bell, attaching them to the cake with a dab of royal icing. Allow the icing to dry, then cover the cake and pack in an airtight tin until needed.

ORANGE SHORTBREAD FINGERS

These are a real tea-time treat. The fingers will keep in an airtight tin for up to two weeks.

INGREDIENTS

115g/4oz/½ cup unsalted butter, softened
50g/2oz/4 tbsp caster sugar, plus a little
extra for sprinkling
finely grated rind of 2 oranges
175g/6oz/1½ cups plain flour

Makes 18

COOK'S TIP

This recipe is the ideal life-saver for busy cooks. It is a good idea to make extra dough and store it, well wrapped, in the freezer. When guests arrive unexpectedly, you will be able to make up freshly-baked fingers in minutes.

1 Preheat the oven to 190°C/375°F/ Gas 5. Beat the butter and sugar together until they are soft and creamy. Beat in the orange rind. Gradually add the flour and gently pull the dough together to form a soft ball.

2 Roll the dough out on a lightly floured surface until about 1cm/½in thick. Cut it into fingers, sprinkle over a little extra sugar, prick with a fork and bake for about 20 minutes, or until the fingers are a light golden colour.

Hogmanay Shortbread

Light, crisp shortbread looks so professional when shaped in a mould,

although you could also shape it by hand.

INGREDIENTS

175g/6oz/¾ cup plain flour
50g/2oz/¼ cup cornflour
50g/2oz/¼ cup caster sugar
115g/4oz/½ cup unsalted butter

Makes 2 large or 8 individual
shortbreads

COOK'S TIP

The secret of successful shortbread baking is to have cool hands when working the butter and sugar together.

1 Preheat the oven to 160°C/325°F/ Gas 3. Lightly flour the mould and line a baking sheet with non-stick baking paper. Sift the flour, cornflour and sugar into a large mixing bowl. Cut the butter into pieces and rub into the flour mixture, using your fingertips or in a food processor. When the mixture begins to bind together, you can knead it into a soft dough, using your hands.

2 Place the dough into the mould and press to fit neatly. Invert the mould on to the baking sheet and tap firmly to release the dough shape. Bake in the preheated oven for about 35–40 minutes or until the shortbread is pale golden in colour.

3 Sprinkle the top of the shortbread with a little caster sugar and set aside to cool on the baking sheet. Wrap the shortbread in cellophane paper and pack in an airtight tin, or place in a box tied with ribbons, to give as a gift.

CHRISTMAS BISCUITS

These biscuits are great fun for children to make as presents. Any shape of biscuit cutter can be used.

Store the biscuits in an airtight tin, and for a change, omit the lemon rind and add 25g/1oz/⅓ cup

of ground almonds and a few drops of almond essence.

INGREDIENTS

75g/3oz/6 tbsp butter
50g/2oz/generous ½ cup icing sugar
finely grated rind of 1 small lemon
1 egg yolk
175g/6oz/1½ cups plain flour
pinch of salt

To Decorate
2 egg yolks
red and green edible food colourings

Makes about 12

1 In a large bowl, beat the butter, sugar and lemon rind together until pale and fluffy. Beat in the egg yolk and then sift in the flour and the salt. Knead together to form a smooth dough. Wrap in clear film and chill for 30 minutes.

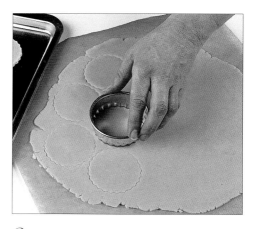

2 Preheat the oven to 190°C/375°F/ Gas 5. On a lightly floured surface, roll out the dough to 3mm/⅛in thick. Using a 6cm/2½in fluted cutter, stamp out as many biscuits as you can, with the cutter dipped in flour to prevent it from sticking to the dough.

3 Transfer the biscuits on to lightly greased baking trays. Mark the tops lightly with a 2.5cm/1in holly leaf cutter and use a 5mm/¼in plain piping nozzle for the berries. Chill for 10 minutes, until firm.

4 Meanwhile, put each egg yolk into a small cup. Mix red food colouring into one and green food colouring into the other. Using a small, clean paintbrush, carefully paint the colours on to the biscuits. Bake the biscuits for 10–12 minutes, or until they begin to colour around the edges. Let them cool slightly on the baking trays, and then transfer them to a wire rack to cool completely.

🌿 COOK'S TIP 🌿

When cooking with young children, things will flow more smoothly if you have all the ingredients prepared before they start to cook. It is a good idea to provide large aprons for all involved!

GINGER FLORENTINES

These colourful, chewy biscuits are delicious served with ice cream and are certain to disappear

as soon as they are served. Store them in an airtight container.

INGREDIENTS

50g/2oz/4 tbsp butter
115g/4oz/8 tbsp caster sugar
50g/2oz/¼ cup chopped mixed glacé cherries
25g/1oz/2 tbsp chopped orange peel
50g/2oz/½ cup flaked almonds
50g/2oz/½ cup chopped walnuts
25g/1oz/1 tbsp chopped glacé ginger
30ml/2 tbsp plain flour
2.5ml/½ tsp ground ginger

To Finish
50g/2oz plain chocolate
50g/2oz white chocolate

Makes 30

1 Preheat the oven to 180°C/350°F/ Gas 4. Whisk together the butter and sugar in a mixing bowl until they are light and fluffy. Thoroughly mix in all the remaining ingredients, except for the chocolate.

2 Cut a piece of non-stick baking paper large enough to fit your baking trays. Put 4 small spoonfuls of the mixture on to each tray, spacing them well apart to allow for spreading. Gently flatten the biscuits with the palm of your hand and bake them for 5 minutes.

3 Remove the biscuits from the oven and flatten them with a wet fork, shaping them into neat rounds. Return to the oven for 3–4 minutes, until they are golden brown.

4 Allow the biscuits to cool on the baking trays for 2 minutes, to firm up, and then, using a palette knife, carefully transfer them to a wire rack. When the biscuits are cold and firm, melt the plain and the white chocolate. Spread dark chocolate on the undersides of half the biscuits and spread white chocolate on the undersides of the rest.

CHOCOLATE KISSES

These rich little biscuits look attractive mixed together on a plate and dusted with icing sugar.

Serve them with ice cream or simply as a sweet accompaniment to coffee.

INGREDIENTS

75g/3oz plain chocolate, broken into squares
75g/3oz white chocolate, broken into squares
115g/4oz/½ cup butter
115g/4oz/8 tbsp caster sugar
2 eggs
225g/8oz/2 cups plain flour
icing sugar, to decorate

Makes 24

3 Halve the mixture and divide it between the two bowls of melted chocolate. Mix the chocolate into the dough mixture thoroughly. Knead the doughs until smooth and pliable, wrap them in clear film and set aside to chill them for about 1 hour. Preheat the oven to 190°C/ 375°F/Gas 5.

4 Shape slightly rounded teaspoonfuls of both doughs roughly into balls. Roll the balls in the palms of your hands to make neater ball shapes. Arrange the balls on greased baking trays and bake them for 10–12 minutes. Dust with sifted icing sugar and then transfer them to a wire rack to cool.

1 Put each pile of chocolate squares into a small bowl and, stirring occasionally, melt it over a pan of hot, but not boiling, water. Set aside to cool.

2 Whisk together the butter and caster sugar until they are pale and fluffy. Gradually beat in the eggs, one at a time. Then sift in the flour and mix together well.

DATE-FILLED PASTRIES

The secret of good pastries is to get as much date filling into the pastry as possible,

but you must make sure to seal the opening well.

INGREDIENTS

75g/3oz/6 tbsp margarine or butter, softened
175g/6oz/1½ cups plain flour
5ml/1 tsp rose water
5ml/1 tsp orange flower water
45ml/3 tbsp water

For the Filling
115g/4oz/⅔ cup stoned dried dates
2.5ml/½ tsp orange flower water
20ml/4 tsp sifted icing sugar for sprinkling

Makes about 25

1 To make the filling, chop the dates finely. Add 50ml/2fl oz/¼ cup boiling water and the orange flower water, beat the mixture and leave to cool.

2 To make the pastries, rub the fat into the flour. Add the flower waters and the water and mix.

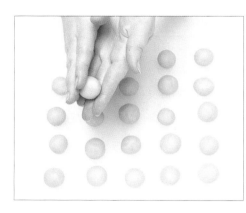

3 Once the dough feels firm, shape it into about 25 small balls.

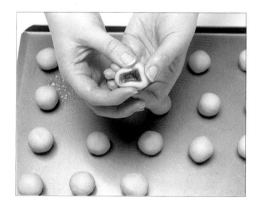

4 Preheat the oven to 180°C/350°F/ Gas 4. Press your finger into each ball to make a small container, pressing the sides round and round to make the walls thinner. Put about 1.5ml/¼ tsp of the date mixture into each one and seal by pressing the pastry together.

5 Arrange the date pastries, seam side down, on a lightly greased baking sheet and prick each one with a fork. Bake in the preheated oven for 15–20 minutes, then transfer to a wire rack and allow to cool completely.

6 Put the cooled pastries on a plate and lightly sprinkle over the sifted icing sugar. Shake gently to make sure they are well covered. Date-filled pastries will freeze very well until needed.

Cinnamon Rolls

These pretty little pastry whirls, scented with cinnamon, are sure to be coffee-time favourites.

INGREDIENTS

For the Dough
400g/14oz/1⅓ cups strong white flour
2.5ml/½ tsp salt
30ml/2 tbsp sugar
5ml/1 tsp easy-blend dried yeast
45ml/3 tbsp oil
1 egg
120ml/4fl oz/½ cup warm milk
120ml/4fl oz/½ cup warm water

For the Filling
25g/1oz butter, softened
25g/1oz soft dark brown sugar
2.5–5ml/½–1 tsp ground cinnamon
15ml/1 tbsp raisins or sultanas

Makes 24 small rolls

1 Sift the flour into a large mixing bowl, the add the salt and sugar and sprinkle over the yeast. Mix together the oil, egg, milk and water and add the liquid to the flour. Mix to a dough, then knead until smooth. Leave the dough to rise until it has doubled in size and then knock it back again.

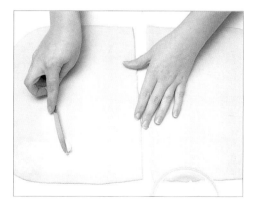

2 Roll out the dough into a large rectangle and cut in half vertically. Spread over the soft butter, reserving 15ml/1 tbsp for brushing. Mix the sugar and cinnamon and sprinkle over the top. Dot with the raisins. Roll each piece of dough into a long Swiss roll shape, to enclose the filling.

3 Cut each piece into 2.5cm/1in slices and arrange on a baking sheet. Brush with butter. Leave to rise for 30 minutes.

4 Preheat the oven to 200°C/400°F/ Gas 6. Bake the rolls for 20 minutes. Leave to cool on a wire rack.

Amaretti

If bitter almonds are not available, make up the weight with sweet almonds.

INGREDIENTS

150g/5oz/1¼ cups sweet almonds
50g/2oz/½ cup bitter almonds
225g/8oz/1 cup caster sugar
2 egg whites
2.5ml/½ tsp almond extract
5ml/1 tsp vanilla extract
icing sugar, for dusting

Makes about 36

1 Preheat the oven to 160°C/325°F/ Gas 3. Peel the almonds by dropping them into a pan of boiling water for 1–2 minutes. Drain. Rub off the skins.

2 Place the almonds on a baking tray and let them dry out in the oven for 10–15 minutes without browning.

3 Grind the almonds with half of the sugar in a food processor. Beat the egg whites until they hold soft peaks. Sprinkle over half the remaining sugar and continue beating until stiff peaks form. Fold in the remaining sugar, almond extract, vanilla and almonds.

4 Spoon the almond mixture into a pastry bag with a smooth nozzle. Line a flat baking sheet with non-stick baking paper. Dust this with flour.

5 Pipe out the mixture in rounds the size of walnuts. Sprinkle lightly with the icing sugar, and allow to stand for 2 hours. Near the end of this time, turn the oven on again and preheat to 180°C/350°F/Gas 4.

6 Bake the amaretti in the preheated oven for 15 minutes, or until they turn pale gold. Remove from the oven and allow them to cool on a rack. When completely cool, the biscuits may be stored in an airtight container.

> #### COOK'S TIP
>
> *Bitter almonds can usually be found in good Italian delicatessens or health food shops.*

Mocha Viennese Swirls

Some temptations just can't be resisted.

Put out a plate of these "melt-in-the-mouth" marvels and watch them vanish.

INGREDIENTS

115g/4oz plain chocolate, broken into squares
200g/7oz/scant 1 cup unsalted butter, softened
50g/2oz/6 tbsp icing sugar
30ml/2tbsp strong black coffee
200g/7oz/1¾ cups plain flour
50g/2oz/½ cup cornflour

To Decorate
about 20 blanched almonds
150g/5oz plain chocolate

Makes about 20

COOK'S TIP

If the mixture is too stiff to pipe, soften it by adding a little more black coffee, a little at a time.

1 Preheat the oven to 190°C/375°F/ Gas 5. Lightly grease two large baking sheets. Melt the chocolate squares in a mixing bowl over hot water. Cream the butter with the icing sugar in a bowl until smooth and pale. Beat in the melted chocolate, then the strong black coffee.

2 Sift the flour and cornflour over the mixture in the bowl. Fold in lightly and evenly to make a soft mixture.

3 Spoon into a piping bag fitted with a large star nozzle and pipe about 20 swirls on the baking sheets.

4 Press an almond into the centre of each of the swirls. Bake for about 15 minutes or until the biscuits are firm and just beginning to brown.

5 Leave the biscuits to cool for about 10 minutes on the baking sheets, then lift them carefully on to a wire rack and allow them to cool completely.

6 When the biscuits have cooled, melt the chocolate and dip the base of each swirl to coat. Place the coated biscuits on a sheet of non-stick baking paper and leave to set.

DOUBLE-CRUST MINCE PIES

Mince pies are an essential part of the culinary tradition and the Christmas season would not be complete without them. This recipe has an extra-special pastry case for maximum delight.

INGREDIENTS

*shortcrust pastry made with 350g/
12oz/3 cups flour
butter, for greasing
flour for dusting
450g/1lb/2 cups mincemeat
milk, for brushing
icing sugar or caster sugar, for dusting*

Makes 24 pies

1 Preheat the oven to 200°C/400°F/ Gas 6. Use a rolling pin to roll out the shortcrust pastry as thinly as possible on a lightly floured board. Using a 7.5cm/3in plain round cutter, cut out 24 circles. With a 5cm/2in plain round cutter, cut out another 24 circles. Carefully lay the circles aside.

2 Grease 24 muffin tins, dust them with flour and line them with the larger circles. Fill each one with mincemeat, then brush the edges with milk. Press the smaller rounds on top and seal the edges. Brush the tops with milk.

3 Bake for 25–30 minutes until the pastry is light golden brown. Cool in the tins, then transfer the pies to a wire rack to become cold. Store them in an airtight tin. Just before serving, dust the tops with sugar. Serve the pies warm.

> ### COOK'S TIP
>
> *Today's mincemeat no longer contains meat or poultry as it once did, except in the form of suet. If you do not wish to eat animal fats, make sure you choose a mincemeat made with vegetarian suet.*

Almond Mincemeat Tartlets

Serve these little tartlets warm with brandy- or rum-flavoured custard.

INGREDIENTS

275g/10oz/2½ cups plain flour
75g/3oz/generous ¾ cup icing sugar
5ml/1 tsp ground cinnamon
175g/6oz/¾ cup butter
50g/2oz/⅔ cup ground almonds
1 egg yolk
45ml/3 tbsp milk
450g/1lb jar mincemeat
15ml/1 tbsp brandy or rum

For the Lemon Sponge Filling
115g/4oz/½ cup butter or margarine
115g/4oz/8 tbsp caster sugar
175g/6oz/1½ cups self-raising flour
2 large eggs
finely grated rind of 1 large lemon

For the Lemon Icing
115g/4oz/1 generous cup icing sugar
15ml/1 tbsp lemon juice

Makes 36

1 For the pastry, sift the flour, icing sugar and cinnamon into a bowl and rub in the butter until it resembles fine breadcrumbs. Add the ground almonds and bind with the egg yolk and milk to a soft dough. Knead the dough until smooth, wrap and chill for 30 minutes.

2 Preheat the oven to 190°C/375°F/Gas 5. On a lightly floured surface, roll out the pastry and cut out 36 fluted rounds with a pastry cutter, to line the tins. Mix the mincemeat with the brandy or rum and put a teaspoonful in each pastry case. Chill in the fridge.

3 For the lemon sponge filling, whisk the butter or margarine, sugar, flour, eggs and lemon rind together until smooth. Spoon on top of the mincemeat, dividing it evenly, and level the tops. Bake for 20–30 minutes, or until golden brown and springy to the touch. Remove and leave to cool on a wire rack.

4 For the lemon icing, sift the icing sugar into a bowl and mix with the lemon juice to form a smooth, thick, coating consistency. Spoon into a piping bag and drizzle a zigzag pattern over each of the tartlets. Alternatively, if you're very short of time, simply dust the tartlets with sifted icing sugar before serving.

De Luxe Mincemeat Tart

The mincemeat can be made up and kept in the fridge for up to two weeks.

It can also be used to make individual mince pies.

INGREDIENTS

225g/8oz/2 cups plain flour
10ml/2 tsp ground cinnamon
50g/2oz/⅔ cup finely ground walnuts
115g/4oz/½ cup butter
50g/2oz/4 tbsp caster sugar, plus extra for dusting
1 egg
2 drops vanilla essence
15ml/1 tbsp cold water

For the Mincemeat
2 dessert apples, peeled, cored and coarsely grated
225g/8oz/1⅓ cups raisins
115g/4oz ready-to-eat dried apricots, chopped
115g/4oz ready-to-eat dried figs or prunes, chopped
225g/8oz green grapes, halved and seeded
50g/2oz/½ cup chopped almonds
finely grated rind of 1 lemon
30ml/2 tbsp lemon juice
30ml/2 tbsp brandy or port
1.5ml/¼ tsp mixed spice
115g/4oz/generous ½ cup soft light brown sugar
25g/1oz/2 tbsp butter, melted

Serves 8

1 To make the pastry, put the flour, cinnamon and walnuts in a food processor. Add the butter and process until the mixture resembles fine breadcrumbs. Turn into a bowl and stir in the sugar. Using a fork, beat the egg with the vanilla essence and water. Gradually stir the egg mixture into the dry ingredients. Gather together with your fingertips to form a soft, pliable dough. Knead briefly on a lightly floured surface until smooth. Then wrap the dough in clear film and chill in the fridge for 30 minutes.

2 Mix all of the mincemeat ingredients together in a large bowl.

3 Cut one-third off the pastry and reserve it for the lattice. Roll out the remainder and use it to line a 23cm/9in, loose-based flan tin. Make a 5mm/¼in rim around the top edge.

4 With a rolling pin, roll off the excess pastry. Fill the case with mincemeat.

5 Roll out the remaining pastry and cut it into 1cm/½in strips. Arrange the strips in a lattice over the top of the pastry, wet the joins and press them together well. Chill for 30 minutes.

6 Preheat the oven to 190°C/375°F/Gas 5. Place a baking sheet in the oven to preheat. Brush the pastry with water and dust it with caster sugar. Bake it on the baking sheet for 30–40 minutes. Transfer to a wire rack and leave to cool for 15 minutes. Then carefully remove the flan tin. Serve warm or cold, with sweetened whipped cream.

COOK'S TIP

Mincemeat will taste even better if it is made at least 4 weeks before Christmas and left in a cool, dry, dark place to mature.

Christmas Treats & Edible Gifts

There's nothing nicer to receive at Christmas-time than a selection of homemade sweets and treats in beautiful festive wrappings. If you're used to shop-bought fudge or Turkish delight, you'll be astounded by the taste of these homemade versions. The same goes for the marshmallow recipe included here, which produces little pillows of mouthwatering delight. Though marzipan fruits and fruit fondant chocolates take a little time and effort, the results will be well worth the trouble. Collections of biscuits and individual cakes are a favourite Christmas treat, as are the Mini Black Buns, hiding their luscious filling inside. Try Flavoured Vinegars and Fruits in Liqueurs for special gifts that taste as good as they look.

CREAMY FUDGE

A good selection of fudge always makes a welcome change from chocolates.

Mix and match the flavours to make a gift-wrapped assortment.

INGREDIENTS

50g/2oz/4 tbsp unsalted butter, plus extra
for greasing
450g/1lb/2 cups granulated sugar
300ml/½ pint/1¼ cups double cream
150ml/¼ pint/⅔ cup milk
45ml/3 tbsp water (this can be replaced
with orange, apricot or cherry brandy,
or strong coffee)

Flavourings
225g/8oz/1 cup plain or milk
chocolate dots
115g/4oz/1 cup chopped almonds,
hazelnuts, walnuts or brazil nuts
115g/4oz/½ cup chopped glacé cherries,
dates or dried apricots

Makes 900g/2lb

1 Grease a 20cm/8in shallow square tin. Place the butter, sugar, cream, milk and water or other flavourings into a large heavy-based saucepan. Heat very gently, until all the sugar has dissolved.

2 Bring the mixture to a rolling boil, until the fudge reaches the soft ball stage.

3 If you are making chocolate-flavoured fudge, add the chocolate dots to the mixture at this stage. Remove the saucepan from the heat and beat thoroughly until the mixture starts to thicken and become opaque.

4 Just before this consistency has been reached, add chopped nuts for a nutty fudge, or glacé cherries or dried fruit for a fruit-flavoured fudge. Beat well until evenly blended.

5 Pour the fudge into the prepared tin, taking care as the mixture is very hot. Leave the mixture until cool and almost set. Using a sharp knife, mark the fudge into small squares and leave in the tin until quite firm.

6 Turn the fudge out on to a board and invert. Using a long-bladed knife, cut into neat squares. You can dust some with icing sugar and drizzle others with melted chocolate, if desired.

ORANGE, MINT AND COFFEE MERINGUES

These tiny, crisp meringues are flavoured with orange, coffee and mint chocolate sticks and liqueurs.

Pile them into dry, airtight glass jars or decorative tins.

INGREDIENTS

25g/1oz/8 chocolate mint sticks
25g/1oz/8 chocolate orange sticks
25g/1oz/8 chocolate coffee sticks
2.5ml/½ tsp crème de menthe
2.5ml/½ tsp orange curaçao or Cointreau
2.5ml/½ tsp Tia Maria
3 egg whites
175g/6oz/¾ cup caster sugar
5g/1 tsp cocoa

Makes 90

COOK'S TIP

These little meringues are ideal served with coffee after dinner. Alternatively, they make an original topping for ice-cream sundaes.

1 Preheat the oven to 110°C/225°F/ Gas ¼. Line 2–3 baking sheets with non-stick baking paper. Chop each flavour of chocolate stick separately and place each into separate bowls, retaining a teaspoonful of each flavour of stick. Stir in the liquid flavourings to match the flavour of the chocolate sticks in the bowls.

2 Place the egg whites in a clean bowl and whisk until stiff. Gradually add the sugar, whisking well after each addition until thick. Add ⅓ of the meringue to each bowl and fold in gently, using a clean spatula, until evenly blended.

3 Place about 30 teaspoons of each mixture on to the baking sheets, spaced apart. Sprinkle the top of each meringue with the reserved chopped chocolate sticks. Bake for 1 hour or until crisp. Allow to cool, then dust with coccoa.

Turkish Delight

Turkish Delight is always a favourite at Christmas, and this versatile recipe can be made in minutes. Try

different flavours such as lemon, crème de menthe and orange and vary the colours accordingly.

INGREDIENTS

450g/1lb/2 cups granulated sugar
300ml/½ pint/1¼ cups water
25g/1oz/2 tbsp powdered gelatine
2.5ml/½ tsp tartaric acid
30ml/2 tbsp rose water
pink food colouring
25g/1oz/3 tbsp icing sugar, sifted
15ml/1 tbsp cornflour

Makes 450g/1lb

1 Wet the insides of 2 x 18cm/7in shallow square tins with water. Place the sugar and all but 60ml/4 tbsp of water into a heavy-based saucepan. Heat gently, stirring occasionally, until the sugar has dissolved.

2 Blend the gelatine and remaining water in a small bowl and place over a saucepan of hot water. Stir occasionally until dissolved. Bring the sugar syrup to the boil and boil steadily for about 8 minutes, or until the syrup registers 127°C/260°F on a sugar thermometer. Stir the tartaric acid into the gelatine, then pour into the boiling syrup and stir until well blended. Remove from the heat.

3 Add the rose water and a few drops of pink food colouring and stir, adding a few more drops, as necessary, to tint the mixture pale pink. Pour the mixture into the prepared tins and allow to set for several hours or overnight. Dust a sheet of greaseproof paper with some of the icing sugar and cornflour. Dip the base of the tins in hot water and invert on to the paper. Cut the Turkish Delight into 2.5cm/1in squares, using an oiled knife. Toss the squares in icing sugar to coat evenly.

GLACÉ FRUITS

These luxury sweetmeats are very popular at Christmas and they cost a fraction of the shop price if

made at home. The preparation is done over about 4 weeks, but the result is well worth the effort.

Choose one type of fruit, or select a variety of fruits such as cherries, plums, peaches, apricots,

starfruit, pineapple, apples, oranges, lemons, limes and clementines.

INGREDIENTS

450g/1lb fruit
1kg/2¼lb/4½ cups granulated sugar
115g/4oz/1 cup powdered glucose

Makes 24 pieces

1 Stone cherries, plums, peaches and apricots. Peel and core pineapple and cut into cubes or rings. Peel, core and quarter apples and thinly slice citrus fruits. Prick cherry skins with a cocktail stick to extract the maximum flavour.

2 Place enough prepared fruit in a saucepan to cover the base, keeping individual fruit types together. Add water to cover the fruit and simmer gently, to avoid breaking it, until almost tender. Use a slotted spoon to transfer the fruit to a shallow dish, removing any skins if necessary. Repeat as above until all the fruit has been cooked.

3 Measure 300ml/½ pint/1¼ cups of the liquid, or make up this quantity with water if necessary. Pour into the saucepan and add 50g/2oz/4 tbsp sugar and the glucose. Heat gently, stirring occasionally, until dissolved. Bring to the boil and pour over the fruit in the dish, completely immersing it, and leave overnight.

4 DAY 2. Drain the syrup into the pan and add 50g/2oz/4 tbsp sugar. Dissolve the sugar and bring to the boil. Pour over the fruit and leave overnight. Repeat this process each day, draining off the syrup, dissolving 50g/2oz/4 tbsp sugar, boiling the syrup and immersing the fruit. Leave overnight on Days 3, 4, 5, 6 and 7.

5 DAY 8. Drain the fruit, dissolve 75g/3oz/½ cup sugar in the syrup and bring to the boil. Add the fruit and cook gently for 3 minutes. Return to the dish and leave for 2 days. DAY 10. Repeat as for Day 8. The syrup should now look like honey. Leave in the dish for at least 10 days, or up to 3 weeks.

6 Place a wire rack over a tray and remove each piece of fruit with a slotted spoon. Arrange on the rack. Dry the fruit in a warm, dry place or in the oven at the lowest setting until the surface no longer feels sticky. To coat in sugar, spear each piece of fruit and plunge into boiling water, then roll in granulated sugar. To dip into syrup, place the remaining sugar and 175ml/6fl oz/¾ cup of water in a saucepan. Heat gently until the sugar has dissolved, then boil for 1 minute. Dip each piece of fruit into boiling water, then quickly into the syrup. Place on the wire rack and leave in a warm place until dry. Place the fruits in paper sweet cases and pack into boxes.

FRUIT FONDANT CHOCOLATES

These chocolates are simple to make using pre-formed plastic moulds, yet they look very professional.

Fruit fondant is available from specialist foods shops and comes in a variety of flavours, including coffee

and nut. Try a mixture of flavours, using a small quantity of each, or use just a single flavour.

INGREDIENTS

225g/8oz/8 squares plain,
milk or white chocolate
115g/4oz/1 cup real fruit liquid fondant
15–20ml/3–4 tsp cooled boiled water

Decoration
15ml/1 tbsp melted plain, milk or white
chocolate

Makes 24

1 Melt the chocolate. Use a piece of cotton wool to polish the insides of the chocolate mouids, ensuring that they are spotlessly clean. Fill up the shapes in one plastic tray to the top, leave for a few seconds, then invert the tray over the bowl of melted chocolate, allowing the excess chocolate to fall back into the bowl. Sit the tray on the work surface and draw a palette knife across the top to remove the excess chocolate and to neaten the edges. Chill until set. Repeat to fill the remaining trays.

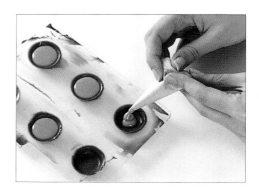

2 Sift the fruit fondant mixture into a bowl. Gradually stir in enough water to give it the consistency of thick cream. Place the fondant in a greaseproof paper piping bag, fold down the top and snip off the end. Fill each chocolate case almost to the top by piping in the fondant. Leave for 30 minutes or until a skin has formed on the surface of the fondant.

3 Spoon the remaining melted chocolate over the fondant to fill each mould level to the top. Chill until the chocolate has set hard. Invert the tray and press out the chocolates one by one. Place the melted chocolate of a contrasting colour into a greaseproof paper piping bag, fold down the top, snip off the point and pipe lines across the top of each chocolate. Allow to set, then pack the chocolates in pretty boxes and tie with ribbon.

CHOCOLATE TRUFFLES

These truffles are a Christmas speciality in France.

They can be rolled in cocoa or nuts, or dipped in chocolate.

INGREDIENTS

175ml/6fl oz/¾ cup double cream
275g/10oz plain chocolate, chopped
25g/1oz/2 tbsp unsalted butter,
cut into pieces
30–45ml/2–3 tbsp brandy (optional)

For the Coating
cocoa powder
finely chopped pistachio nuts or hazelnuts
400g/14oz plain, milk or white chocolate

Makes 20–30

1 Bring the cream to the boil. Remove from the heat and add the chocolate, then stir until melted. Stir in the butter and the brandy, if using, then strain into a bowl and cool. Cover and chill overnight.

2 Line a large baking sheet with greaseproof paper. Using two teaspoons, form the chocolate mixture into 20–30 balls and place on the paper. Chill if the mixture becomes soft.

3 To coat the truffles with cocoa, sift the cocoa into a bowl, drop in the truffles, one at a time, and roll to coat well, keeping the round shape. To coat with nuts, roll truffles in finely chopped nuts. Chill, wrapped, for up to 10 days.

4 To coat the truffles with chocolate, freeze the truffles for at least 1 hour. In a small bowl, melt the plain, milk or white chocolate over a saucepan of barely simmering water, stirring until the chocolate has melted and is smooth, then allow to cool slightly.

5 Using a fork, dip the frozen truffles into the cooled chocolate, one at a time, tapping the fork on the edge of the bowl to shake off the excess. Place on a baking sheet lined with non-stick baking paper and chill at once. If the melted chocolate thickens, reheat until smooth. Wrap in clear film and store in a cool place for up to 10 days.

MARSHMALLOWS

These light and fragrant mouthfuls of pale pink mousse are flavoured with rose water.

INGREDIENTS

oil, for greasing
45ml/3 tbsp icing sugar
45ml/3 tbsp cornflour
50ml/2fl oz/¼ cup cold water
45ml/3 tbsp rose water
25g/1oz/1 tbsp powdered gelatine
pink food colouring
450g/1lb/2 cups granulated sugar
30ml/2 level tbsp liquid glucose
250ml/8fl oz/1 cup boiling water
2 egg whites

Makes 500g/1¼lb

1 Lightly oil a 28 x 18cm/11 x 7in Swiss roll tin. Sift together the icing sugar and cornflour and use some to coat the inside of the tin.

2 Mix the cold water, rose water, gelatine and a drop of food colouring in a bowl. Place over a pan of hot water. Stir until the gelatine has dissolved.

3 Place the sugar, liquid glucose and boiling water in a heavy-based saucepan. Stir to dissolve the sugar.

4 Bring the syrup to the boil and boil steadily without stirring until the temperature reaches 127°C/260°F on a sugar thermometer. Remove from the heat and stir in the gelatine mixture.

5 While the syrup is boiling, whisk the egg whites stiffly in a large bowl using an electric hand whisk. Pour a steady stream of syrup on to the egg whites while whisking continuously for about 3 minutes, until the mixture is thick and foamy. At this stage add more food colouring, if the mixture looks too pale.

6 Pour the mixture into the prepared tin and allow to set for about 4 hours or overnight. Sift some of the remaining icing sugar mixture over the surface of the marshmallow and the rest over a board or baking sheet. Ease the mixture away from the tin using an oiled palette knife and invert on to the board. Cut into 2.5cm/1in squares, coating the cut sides with the icing sugar mixture. Pack the marshmallows into glass containers or tins and seal well.

MARZIPAN FRUITS

These eye-catching and realistic fruits will make a perfect gift for lovers of marzipan.

INGREDIENTS

450g/1lb white marzipan
yellow, green, red, orange and burgundy
food colouring dusts
30g/1½oz/2 tbsp whole cloves

Makes 450g/1lb

1 Cover a baking sheet with non-stick baking paper. Cut the marzipan into quarters. Take 1 piece and cut it into 10 even-size pieces. Place a little of each of the food colouring dusts into a food paint palette, or place small amounts spaced apart on a plate. Cut ⅔ of the cloves into 2 pieces, making a stem and core end.

2 Shape the 10 pieces into a neat ball. Dip 1 ball into the yellow food colouring and roll to colour. Re-dip into the green colouring and re-roll to tint a greeny-yellow colour. Roll one end to make a pear shape. Press a clove stem into the top and a core end into the base. Repeat with the remaining balls. Place on the prepared baking sheet.

3 Cut another piece of the marzipan into 10 pieces and shape into neat balls. Dip each piece of marzipan into the green food colouring dust and roll in the palms to colour evenly. Add a spot of red colouring dust and roll gently to blend the colour. Using a ball tool or the end of a fine paint-brush, indent the top and base to make an apple shape. Make a stem and core, using cloves.

4 Repeat as above, using another piece of the marzipan to make 10 orange coloured balls. Roll each over the surface of a fine grater to give the texture of an orange skin. Press a clove core into the base of each.

5 Take the remaining piece of marzipan, reserve a small piece, and mould the rest into lots of tiny marzipan beads. Colour them burgundy with the food colouring. Place a whole clove on the baking sheet. Arrange a cluster of burgundy beads in the shape of a bunch of grapes. Repeat with the remaining burgundy beads of marzipan to make another 3 bunches of grapes.

6 Roll out the remaining piece of marzipan thinly and brush with green food colouring. Using a vine leaf cutter, cut out 8 leaves, mark the veins with a knife and place 2 on each bunch of grapes. Leave the fruits to dry, then pack into gift boxes.

PEPPERMINT CHOCOLATE STICKS

These delicious bite-size chocolate sticks will prove irresistible.

INGREDIENTS

115g/4oz/½ cup granulated sugar
150ml/¼ pint/⅔ cup water
2.5ml/½ tsp peppermint essence
*200g/7oz plain dark chocolate, broken
into squares*
60ml/4 tbsp toasted desiccated coconut

Makes about 80

1 Lightly oil a large baking sheet.
Place the sugar and water in a small
heavy-based saucepan over a medium-
low heat. Allow the water to heat gently,
until the sugar has dissolved completely.
Stir occasionally.

2 Bring to the boil and boil rapidly until
the syrup registers 138°C/280°F on a sugar
thermometer. Remove from the heat. Add
the peppermint essence and pour on to
the greased baking sheet. Leave to set.

3 Break up the peppermint mixture
into a small bowl and use the end of a
rolling pin to crush it into small pieces.

4 Melt the chocolate in a heatproof
bowl over hot water. Remove from the
heat and stir in the mint pieces and
desiccated coconut.

5 Spread the chocolate mixture over
a 30 x 25cm/12 x 10in sheet of non-stick
baking paper, to make a rectangle
measuring about 25 x 20cm/10 x 8in.
Leave to set. When firm, use a sharp
knife to cut into thin sticks, each about
6cm/2½in long.

TRUFFLE CHRISTMAS PUDDINGS

Truffles disguised as Christmas puddings are great fun both to make and receive.

Make any flavour truffles, and decorate them as you like.

INGREDIENTS

20 plain chocolate truffles
15ml/1 tbsp cocoa
15ml/1 tbsp icing sugar
225g/8oz/1 cup white chocolate dots,
melted
50g/2oz/¼ cup white marzipan
green and red food colourings
yellow food colouring dust

Makes 20

COOK'S TIP

These little truffle puddings are fun to make at home and children will love to help. They may be able to coat the truffles, do some stamping, or pack the finished puddings in a box as a special present.

1 Make the truffles following the recipe on page 227. Sift the cocoa and icing sugar together and coat the truffles.

2 Spread ⅔ of the white chocolate over a piece of non-stick baking paper. Using a small daisy cutter, stamp out 20 rounds. Place a truffle on the centre of each daisy shape, secured with a little of the reserved melted chocolate.

3 Colour ⅔ of the marzipan green and ⅓ red using the food colourings. Roll out the green marzipan thinly and stamp out 40 leaves, using a tiny holly leaf cutter. Mark the veins with a sharp knife. Mould lots of tiny red marzipan beads. Colour the remaining white chocolate with yellow food colouring dust and place in a greaseproof paper piping bag. Fold down the top of the bag, cut off the point and pipe the marzipan over the top of each truffle to resemble custard. Arrange the holly leaves and berries on the top of the puddings. When the truffle puddings have set, arrange them in gift boxes, label and tie with ribbon.

Striped Biscuits

Eat these biscuits with scoops of vanilla ice cream or any light desserts.

INGREDIENTS

25g/1oz/1 square white chocolate, melted
red and green food colouring dusts
2 egg whites
90g/3½oz/⅓ cup caster sugar
50g/2oz/½ cup plain flour
50g/2oz/4 tbsp unsalted butter, melted

Makes 25

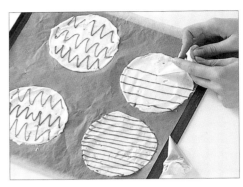

1 Preheat the oven to 190°C/375°F/Gas 5. Line 2 baking sheets with non-stick baking paper. Divide the melted chocolate in two and use the food colouring dust to colour the chocolate red and green. Fill 2 greaseproof paper piping bags with each chocolate and fold down the tops. Snip off the points.

2 Place the egg whites in a mixing bowl and whisk until they form stiff peaks. Gradually add the sugar to the bowl, whisking well after each addition, to make a thick meringue. Sift in the flour and melted butter and whisk some more until the mixture is smooth.

3 Drop 4 separate teaspoonfuls of mixture on to the baking sheets and spread into thin rounds. Pipe lines or zigzags of green and red chocolate over each round. Bake in the oven for 3–4 minutes or until pale golden in colour. Loosen the rounds with a palette knife and return to the oven for a few seconds to soften. Have ready 2 or 3 lightly oiled wooden spoon handles at hand.

4 Taking one biscuit out of the oven at a time, roll it around a spoon handle and leave it for a few seconds to set. Repeat to shape the remaining biscuits.

5 When the biscuits are set, leave on a wire rack to cool. Repeat with the remaining mixture and the red and green chocolate until all the mixture has been used.

6 When the biscuits are cold, tie them together with a length of brightly coloured ribbon and pack into airtight boxes, tins or glass jars.

MACAROONS

These little macaroons can be served as petit-fours with coffee.

Dust with icing sugar or cocoa before serving.

INGREDIENTS

50g/2oz/⅔ cup ground almonds
50g/2oz/¼ cup caster sugar
15ml/1 tbsp cornflour
1.5–2.5ml/¼–½ tsp almond essence
1 egg white, whisked
15 flaked almonds
4 glacé cherries, quartered
icing sugar or cocoa, to dust

Makes 30

COOK'S TIP

To make chocolate-flavoured macaroons, replace the cornflour with the same amount of cocoa powder.

1 Preheat the oven to 160°C/325°F/Gas 3. Line 2 baking sheets with non-stick baking paper. Place the ground almonds, sugar, cornflour and almond essence into a bowl and mix together well, using a wooden spoon.

2 Stir in just enough egg white to form a soft piping consistency. Place the mixture into a nylon piping bag fitted with a 1cm/½in plain piping nozzle.

3 Pipe about 15 rounds of mixture on to each baking sheet, spaced well apart. Press a flaked almond on to half the macaroons and glacé cherries on to the remainder. Bake for 10–15 minutes.

Individual Dundee Cakes

Dundee cakes are traditionally topped with almonds but also look tempting covered with glacé fruits.

Ingredients

225g/8oz/1 cup raisins
225g/8oz/1 cup currants
225g/8oz/1 cup sultanas
50g/2oz/¼ cup sliced glacé cherries
115g/4oz/¾ cup mixed peel
grated rind of 1 orange
300g/11oz/2¾ cups plain flour
2.5ml/½ tsp baking powder
5ml/1 tsp mixed spice
225g/8oz/1 cup unsalted butter, softened
225g/8oz/1 cup caster sugar
5 eggs

Topping

50g/2oz/½ cup whole blanched almonds
50g/2oz/¼ cup halved glacé cherries
50g/2oz/½ cup sliced glacé fruits
45ml/3 tbsp apricot glaze

Makes 3

1 Preheat the oven to 150°C/300°F/ Gas 2. Prepare 3 x 15cm/6in round cake tins. Place all the fruit and the orange rind into a large mixing bowl. Mix together until blended. In another bowl, sift the flour, baking powder and mixed spice. Add the butter, sugar and eggs. Mix together and beat for 2–3 minutes until smooth and glossy. Alternatively use a food mixer or processor for 1 minute.

2 Add the mixed fruit to the cake mixture and fold in, using a spatula, until blended. Divide the cake mixture between the 3 tins and level the tops. Arrange the almonds in circles over the top of one cake, the glacé cherries over the second cake and the mixed glacé fruits over the last one. Bake in the oven for approximately 2–2½ hours or until a skewer inserted into the centre of the cakes comes out clean.

3 Leave the cakes in their tins until completely cold. Turn out, remove the paper and brush the tops with apricot glaze. Leave to set, then wrap in cellophane paper or clear film and place in pretty boxes.

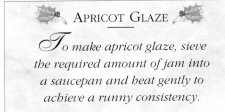

Apricot Glaze

To make apricot glaze, sieve the required amount of jam into a saucepan and heat gently to achieve a runny consistency.

Mini Black Buns

This is a traditional Scottish recipe with a rich fruit cake mixture cooked inside a bun dough.

INGREDIENTS

*50g/2oz/4 tbsp butter, melted, plus extra
for brushing
225g/8oz/1 cup mixed dried fruit
50g/2oz/¼ cup glacé cherries, chopped
50g/2oz/½ cup chopped almonds
10ml/2 tsp grated lemon rind
25g/1oz/2 tbsp caster sugar
15ml/1 tbsp whisky
50g/2oz/½ cup plain flour
5ml/1 tsp mixed spice
1 egg, beaten*

*Decoration
30ml/2 tbsp apricot glaze (see Introduction)
450g/1lb white marzipan
purple and green food colourings*

Makes 4

1 Preheat the oven to 150°C/300°F/ Gas 2. Cut out 4 x 15cm/6in squares of greaseproof paper and 4 squares of foil. Place the greaseproof paper squares on top of the foil squares and brush with a little melted butter.

2 Place the dried fruit, chopped glacé cherries, chopped almonds, lemon rind, caster sugar, whisky, sifted flour and mixed spice into a large mixing bowl. Using a wooden spoon, stir until all of the ingredients are well mixed. Add the melted butter and egg and beat together until the mixture is well blended.

3 Divide the mixture between the 4 paper and foil squares, draw up the edges to the centre of the foil and twist the squares to mould the mixture into rounds. Place on a baking sheet and bake in the preheated oven for 45 minutes, or until the mixture feels firm when touched. Remove the foil and bake for a further 15 minutes. Open the paper and allow the cakes to cool on a wire rack.

4 Remove the paper and brush each cake with apricot glaze. Cut off ¼ of the marzipan for decoration and put to one side. Cut the remainder into 4 pieces.

5 Roll out each piece of marzipan thinly and cover the cakes. Roll each cake in the palm of your hands to make them into round shapes. Prepare a hot grill and place the cakes on to a baking sheet lined with foil.

6 Grill the cakes until the marzipan is evenly browned. Leave until cold. Colour ½ of the remaining marzipan purple and ½ green with food colourings. Cut out 4 purple thistle shapes, green leaves and stems and arrange them on top of each cake, moistening with a little water to stick. Wrap in cellophane and place into small cake boxes.

FLAVOURED VINEGARS

Flavoured vinegars look extra special if you pour them into beautifully shaped bottles.

INGREDIENTS

*good quality white and red wine vinegar
or cider vinegar*

Herb Vinegar
*15ml/1 tbsp mixed peppercorns
2 lemon slices
4 garlic cloves
rosemary, thyme, tarragon and curry
plant sprigs*

Spice Vinegar
*15ml/1 tbsp allspice berries
2 mace blades
10ml/2 tsp star anise
2 cinnamon sticks
1 orange*

Fruit Vinegar
*450g/1lb/3 cups raspberries
450g/1lb/3 cups gooseberries
450g/1lb/3 cups blackberries or
elderberries*

Makes 600ml/1 pint/2½ cups
of each flavour

1 Sterilize 2 bottles with corks or caps. To the first bottle add the peppercorns, lemon slices and garlic cloves. Place the herb sprigs together and trim the stems so they vary in length. Insert them into the bottle, placing the short ones in first.

2 Into the second bottle add the allspice berries, mace, star anise and cinnamon sticks. Cut 2 slices from the orange and insert into the bottle. Pare the rind from the remaining orange and insert into the bottle.

3 Using white wine vinegar, fill the bottle containing the herbs up to the neck. Repeat to fill the bottle containing the spices with red wine vinegar. Cork or cap the bottles and store them in a cool place.

4 Wash the raspberries, gooseberries and blackberries or elderberries separately under cold running water and place them into separate bowls. Crush the fruit with a wooden spoon.

5 Pour each fruit into a separate clean wide-necked jar and add 600ml/1 pint/ 2½ cups of white wine vinegar. Cover the jars and leave for 3–4 days in a cool place. Shake the jars occasionally to mix well.

6 Strain each fruit separately through a jelly bag or a muslin-lined sieve into a stainless steel saucepan and boil for 10 minutes. Pour into sterilized bottles or jars and seal with lids or tops with plastic-coated linings. All the vinegars should be used within 6 months.

PEPPERS IN OLIVE OIL

The wonderful flavour and colour of these peppers will add a Mediterranean

theme to festive meals. Bottle the peppers separately or mix the colours together.

INGREDIENTS

3 red peppers
3 yellow peppers
3 green peppers
300ml/½ pint/1¼ cups olive oil
2.5ml/½ tsp salt
2.5ml/½ tsp freshly ground black pepper
3 thyme sprigs

Makes enough to fill 3 x 450g/1lb jars

COOK'S TIP

This pungent oil should be stored in a cool, dark place and used within a week. The filled bottles also make great decorations for the home, if you choose not to use the oil for cooking.

1 Prepare a hot grill or preheat the oven to 200°C/400°F/Gas 6. Put the whole peppers on a grill rack or on to a baking sheet. Place under the grill or in the oven and cook for about 10 minutes, until the skins are charred and blistered all over. Turn the peppers frequently during the cooking time.

2 Allow the peppers to cool for at least 5 minutes, then peel off the skins. Remove the cores, seeds and stalks. Slice each of the peppers thinly, keeping each colour separate, and place each into a separate dish.

3 Pour ⅓ of the olive oil over each of the peppers. Season and add a sprig of thyme. Stir well. Sterilize 3 jars and lids and fill each with a mixture of peppers. Top up each jar with the oil. Screw the jar lids on firmly and label.

Fresh Fruit Preserve

The wonderfully fresh flavour of this fruit spread makes it a welcome gift. To vary the recipe,

use a mixture of soft fruits or other individual fruits such as strawberries or blackberries.

INGREDIENTS

675g/1½lb/3½ cups raspberries
900g/2lb/4 cups caster sugar
30ml/2 tbsp lemon juice
120ml/4fl oz/½ cup liquid pectin

Makes 900g/2lb

COOK'S TIP

The process of leaving the fruit in the sugar for an hour is known as macerating. This process allows the fruit to become very pulpy and sweet, with a more intense flavour.

1 Place the raspberries in a large bowl and lightly crush with a wooden spoon. Stir in the caster sugar. Leave for 1 hour at room temperature, giving the mixture an occasional stir to dissolve the sugar.

2 Sterilize several small jars or containers and their lids, if being used. Add the lemon juice and liquid pectin to the raspberries and stir until thoroughly blended.

3 Spoon the raspberry mixture into the jars, leaving a 1cm/½in space at the top if the preserve is to be frozen. Cover the surface of each preserve with a greaseproof paper disc, and cover with the jar lid or with cellophane paper and an elastic band. Do not use a screw-topped lid if the preserve is to be frozen. Allow to cool, then label. The preserve can be stored in the freezer for up to 6 months, or refrigerated for up to 4 weeks.

FRUITS IN LIQUEURS

These eye-catching fruits in liqueurs are best made when the fruits are plentiful, cheap and in season.

Choose from apricots, clementines, kumquats, physalis, cherries, raspberries, peaches, plums or seedless

grapes, and team them with rum, brandy, Kirsch or Cointreau, to name just a few.

INGREDIENTS

450g/1lb/3 cups fresh fruit
225g/8oz/1 cup granulated sugar
150ml/¼ pint/⅔ cup liqueur or spirits

Makes 450g/1lb

5 Boil the syrup rapidly until it reaches 107°C/225°F, or the thread stage. Test by pressing a small amount of syrup between 2 teaspoons; when they are pulled apart, a thread should form. Allow to cool.

6 Measure the cooled syrup, then add an equal quantity of liqueur or spirit. Mix until blended. Pour over the fruit in the jars until covered. Seal each jar with a screw or clip top, label and keep for up to 4 months.

1 Wash the fruit, halve and stone apricots, plums or peaches. Peel back and remove the husk from physalis, hull strawberries or raspberries, and prick kumquats, cherries or grapes all over with a cocktail stick. Pare the rind from clementines using a sharp knife, taking care not to leave any of the bitter white pith.

2 Place 115g/4oz/½ cup of the sugar and 300ml/½ pint/1¼ cups of water into a large saucepan. Heat gently, stirring occasionally, until the sugar has dissolved. Bring to the boil.

3 Add the fruit to the syrup and simmer gently for 1–2 minutes until the fruit is just tender, but the skins are still intact and the fruits are whole.

4 Carefully remove the fruit using a slotted spoon and arrange neatly in the warmed sterilized jars. Add the remaining sugar to the syrup in the saucepan and stir continuously until it has dissolved.

Festive Drinks & Cocktails

*T*he cheerful custom of the Christmas "wassail" –
a steaming bowl of ale mixed with roasted apples, sugar
and spices – has existed for centuries as a celebration of
good cheer. The modern equivalent to this traditional toast
is the ever-popular Mulled Claret, and there are plenty of
other tempting alcoholic and non-alcoholic alternatives
included in this chapter. Brandied Eggnog is one of the
more warming recipes to lift the spirits and, along with
Irish Chocolate Velvet, it makes the ultimate nightcap.
Cocktail drinks such as Buck's Fizz and Cranberry Kiss
are perfect to get the party started, while for the post-party
breakfast, choose the delightful, sparkling Cranberry Frost.

CRANBERRY FROST

A non-alcoholic cocktail with the colour of holly berries will delight younger and older guests alike.

It is the perfect "one-for-the-road" drink to serve at the end of a gathering.

INGREDIENTS

115g/4oz/½ cup caster sugar
juice of 2 oranges
still water, enough to dissolve the sugar
1 litre/1¾ pints/4 cups sparkling mineral water
100ml/4fl oz/½ cup cranberry juice
fresh cranberries, to decorate
sprigs of mint, to decorate

Serves 10

1 Put the sugar, orange juice and still water into a small pan and stir over a low heat to dissolve the sugar. Bring to the boil and boil for 3 minutes. Set aside to cool. The syrup can be made in advance and stored in a covered container in the refrigerator. Pour the syrup into a chilled bowl, pour on the cranberry juice and mix well. To serve, pour on the mineral water and decorate with cranberries and mint leaves.

COOK'S TIP

To make this fabulous non-alcoholic drink the very essence of festive colour, chill with ice cubes made by freezing fresh red cranberries and tiny mint leaves in the water.

MULLED CLARET

This mull is a blend of claret, cider and orange juice. It can be varied to suit the occasion

by increasing or decreasing the proportion of fruit juice or, to give the mull more pep,

by adding up to 150ml/¼ pint/⅔ cup brandy.

INGREDIENTS

1 orange
75ml/5 tbsp clear honey
30ml/2 tbsp seedless raisins
2 clementines
a few cloves
whole nutmeg
60ml/4 tbsp demerara sugar
2 cinnamon sticks
1½ litres/2½ pints/6¼ cups inexpensive claret
600ml/1 pint/2½ cups medium cider
300ml/½ pint/1¼ cups orange juice

Makes 16 x 150ml/¼ pint/⅔ cup glasses

1 With a sharp knife or a rotary peeler, pare off a long strip of orange peel.

2 Place the orange peel, honey and raisins in a large pan. Stud the clementines all over with the cloves and add them to the saucepan.

3 Grate a little nutmeg into the sugar and then add it to the pan with the cinnamon sticks. Pour on the wine and heat over a low heat, stirring until the sugar has completely dissolved and the honey melted.

4 Pour the cider and the orange juice into the saucepan and continue to heat the mull over a gentle heat. Do not allow it to boil or all the alcohol will evaporate.

5 Warm a punch bowl or other large serving bowl. Remove the clementines and cinnamon sticks from the saucepan and strain the mull into the bowl to remove the raisins. Add the clementines studded with cloves, and serve the mull hot, in warmed glasses or in glasses containing a silver spoon (to prevent the glass breaking). Using a nutmeg grater, add a little nutmeg over each serving, if you wish.

BRANDIED EGGNOG

This frothy blend of eggs, milk and spirits definitely comes into the nightcap category of drinks.

INGREDIENTS

4 eggs, separated
30ml/2 tbsp caster sugar
60ml/4 tbsp dark rum
60ml/4 tbsp brandy
*300ml/½ pint/1¼ cups milk (or according
to the volume of the glasses), hot
whole nutmeg*

Serves 4

1 Beat the egg yolks with the sugar. Beat the whites to soft peaks. Mix and pour into 4 heatproof glasses.

2 Pour on the rum and brandy, 15ml/ 1 tbsp of each in each glass.

3 Top up the glass with hot milk. Grate the nutmeg over the top and serve at once.

COOK'S TIP

*You can also make a cold
version of this drink using chilled
single cream instead of the hot milk.*

Irish Chocolate Velvet

This smooth, sophisticated drink will always be appreciated on cold Christmas evenings.

INGREDIENTS

120ml/4fl oz/½ cup double cream
400ml/14fl oz/1⅔ cups milk
30ml/2 tbsp cocoa powder
115g/4oz milk chocolate, broken into squares
60ml/4 tbsp Irish whisky
whipped cream, for topping
chocolate curls, to decorate

Serves 4

COOK'S TIP

If Irish whisky is not available, use brandy or any liqueur which uses whisky or brandy as its base.

1 Whip the cream in a bowl until it is thick enough to hold its shape.

2 Put the milk into a saucepan and whisk in the cocoa powder. Add the chocolate squares and heat gently, stirring, until the chocolate has melted. Bring the chocolate milk to the boil.

3 Remove the saucepan from the heat and add the whipped double cream and Irish whisky. Stir gently for about 1 minute to blend well.

4 Pour quickly into four heatproof mugs or glasses and top each serving with a generous spoonful of whipped cream. Decorate with chocolate curls and serve at once.

Buck's Fizz (Mimosa)

This delightfully refreshing drink, invented by the barman at the Buck's Club in

London in 1921, has achieved star status. In France it is known as "Champagne-orange"

and in Italy and the United States as "Mimosa".

INGREDIENTS

120ml/4fl oz/½ cup fresh orange juice
5ml/1 tsp grenadine syrup
175ml/6fl oz/¾ cup Champagne or other
sparkling white wine, chilled

Makes 1 glass

1 Put the orange juice into a chilled long-stemmed glass. Add the grenadine syrup and stir with a long-handled spoon to blend. Then add the Champagne or white wine and stir again. Serve the cocktail at once, decorated with a slice of fresh orange.

COOK'S TIP

Buck's Fizz, with its refreshing combination of fruit juice and white wine, makes the perfect cocktail drink for Christmas morning.

BRANDY ALEXANDER

A warming digestif, made from a blend of crème de cacao, brandy and double cream,

that can be served at the end of the meal with coffee.

INGREDIENTS

crushed ice
20ml/1 measure/1½ tbsp brandy
20ml/1 measure/1½ tbsp
crème de cacao
20ml/1 measure/1½ tbsp double cream
whole nutmeg, grated, to decorate

Serves 1

VARIATION

Warm the brandy and double cream and whizz in a blender with crème de cacao, until frothy. Serve in a tall glass with a cinnamon stick.

3 Strain the chilled cocktail into a small wine glass.

4 Finely grate a little nutmeg over the top of the cocktail and serve at once.

1 Half fill the cocktail shaker with ice and pour in the brandy, crème de cacao and, finally, the cream.

2 Ensure the lid is screwed firmly in place and shake for about 20 seconds, to mix the ingredients together well.

CRANBERRY KISS

A delicious full-flavoured cocktail, with the tang of cranberry and pink

grapefruit juices and the sweetness of Marsala.

INGREDIENTS

redcurrant string, to decorate
1 egg white, lightly beaten, to decorate
15ml/½oz caster sugar, to decorate
crushed ice
45ml/2 measures/3 tbsp cranberry juice
20ml/1 measure/1½ tbsp brandy
45ml/2 measures/3 tbsp pink grapefruit
juice
45ml/2 measures/3 tbsp Marsala

Serves 1

1 Lightly brush the redcurrants with the egg white.

2 Shake caster sugar over the redcurrants, to cover them in a light frosting. Set them aside to dry.

3 Place the cranberry juice with the brandy and grapefruit juice in a cocktail shaker full of crushed ice and shake for 20 seconds to mix thoroughly.

4 Strain the cocktail mixture into a well-chilled glass.

5 Tilt the glass slightly before slowly pouring the Marsala down the side of the glass into the drink.

6 Serve the cocktail decorated with the frosted redcurrant string.

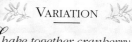

VARIATION
Shake together cranberry and pineapple juice with coconut milk. Add vodka or gin to taste.

FRUIT AND GINGER ALE

An old English mulled drink, served chilled over ice. It can be made with

ready-squeezed apple and orange juices, but roasting the fruit with cloves gives a far superior flavour.

INGREDIENTS

1 cooking apple
1 orange, scrubbed
1 lemon, scrubbed
20 whole cloves
7.5cm/3in fresh root ginger, peeled
25ml/1½ tbsp soft brown sugar
350ml/12fl oz bitter lemon or non-
alcoholic wine
wedges of orange rind and whole cloves,
to decorate

Serves 4–6

1 Preheat the oven to 200°C/400°F/ Gas 6. Score the apple around the middle and stud the orange and lemon with the cloves. Bake them in the oven for 25 minutes until soft and cooked.

2 Quarter the orange and lemon and pulp the apple, discarding the skin and the core. Finely grate the ginger. Place the fruit and ginger together in a bowl with the soft brown sugar.

3 Add 300ml/½ pint/1¼ cups boiling water. Using a spoon, squeeze the fruit to release more flavour. Cover the mixing bowl and leave to cool for several hours or overnight.

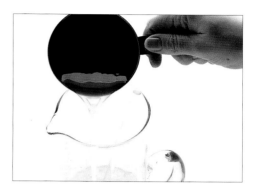

4 Strain into a jug of cracked ice and use a spoon to press out all the juices from the fruit. Add the bitter lemon or non-alcoholic wine to taste. Decorate with orange rind and cloves.

CHRISTMAS SPIRIT

This colourful drink has a sharp but sweet taste. It is excellent served as a winter warmer

or after a meal, but it also makes a good summer drink served with crushed ice.

INGREDIENTS

450g/1lb/2 cups cranberries
2 clementines
450g/1lb/2 cups granulated sugar
1 cinnamon stick
475ml/16fl oz/2 cups vodka

Makes 750ml/1¼ pints/3 cups

1 Crush the cranberries in a food processor and spoon into a large jar. Pare the rind from the clementines and add.

2 Squeeze the juice from the clementines and add to the cranberries and pared rind in the jar. Add the sugar, cinnamon stick and vodka to the jar and seal with the lid or a double thickness of plastic, and tie down securely. Shake the jar well to combine all the ingredients.

3 Store the jar in a cool place for 1 month, shaking the jar daily for 2 weeks, then occasionally. When the drink has matured, sterilize some small pretty bottles and, using a funnel with a filter paper inside, strain the liquid into the bottles and cork immediately. Label the bottles clearly and tie a gift tag around the neck.

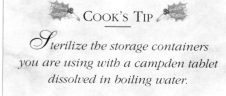

COOK'S TIP

Sterilize the storage containers you are using with a campden tablet dissolved in boiling water.

FESTIVE LIQUEURS

These are easier to make than wines and may be made with a variety of flavours and spirits.

All these liqueurs should be allowed to mature for 3 months before drinking.

INGREDIENTS

Plum Brandy
450g/1lb plums
225g/8oz/1 cup demerara sugar
600ml/1 pint/2½ cups brandy

Fruit Gin
450g/1lb/3 cups raspberries,
blackcurrants or sloes
350g/12oz/1½ cups granulated sugar
750ml/1¼ pints/3 cups gin

Citrus Whisky
1 large orange
1 small lemon
1 lime
225g/8oz/1 cup granulated sugar
600ml/1 pint/2½ cups whisky

Makes 900ml/1½ pints/3¾ cups
of each liqueur

1 Sterilize 3 jars and lids. Wash and halve the plums, remove the stones and slice. Place the plums in the sterilized jar with the sugar and brandy. Crack 3 of the plum stones, remove the kernels and chop. Add them to the jar and stir until blended.

2 Place the raspberries, blackcurrants or sloes into the prepared jar. If using sloes, prick the surface of the berries using a stainless steel pin to extract the flavour. Add the sugar and gin to the jar and stir until the mixture is well blended.

3 To make the Citrus Whisky, first scrub the fruit. Using a sharp knife or potato peeler, pare the rind from the fruit, taking care not to include the white pith. Squeeze out all of the juice and place in the jar with the fruit rinds. Add the sugar and whisky, and stir until well blended.

4 Cover the jars with lids or double thickness plastic tied down well. Store the jars in a cool, dark place for 3 months.

5 Shake the Fruit Gin every day for 1 month, and then occasionally. Shake the Plum Brandy and Citrus Whisky every day for 2 weeks, then occasionally. Sterilize the chosen bottles and corks or stoppers for each liqueur.

6 When each liqueur is ready to be bottled, strain the liquid through a sieve, then pour it into sterilized bottles through a funnel fitted with a filter paper. Fit the corks or stoppers and label the bottles with a festive label.

Suggested Menus

Christmas Dinner
for 8 People

Roquefort Tartlets

*Roast Turkey, stuffing balls, chipolata sausages,
bacon rolls and gravy*

Festive Brussels Sprouts

Traditional Christmas Pudding

Vegetarian Christmas Dinner
for 8 People

Christmas Salad with bought mini bread rolls

Cheese and Spinach Flan or Vegetarian Christmas Pie

Garden Vegetable Terrine or Festive Brussels Sprouts

Crunchy Apple and Almond Flan

Boxing Day Lunch
for 12 People

Warm Prawn Salad with bought herb and garlic bread

Baked Gammon with Cumberland Sauce

Vegetable Gnocchi

De Luxe Mincemeat Tart

Hot Fork Supper
for 12 People

Roquefort Tartlets and Filo Vegetable Pie

Chicken with Red Wine Vinegar

Sweet and Sour Red Cabbage

Iced Praline Torte and Ruby Fruit Salad

Cold Buffet Lunch
for 12 People

Layered Salmon Terrine

Fillet of Beef with Ratatouille

Turkey Rice Salad

*Ginger Trifle and Almond
Mincemeat Tartlets*

New Year's Eve Party
for 8 People

Smoked Salmon Salad

Roast Goose with Caramelized Apples

Gratin Dauphinois and Sweet and Sour Red Cabbage

Chocolate and Chestnut Yule Log

INDEX

A

Advent candle ring, 9
almonds: almond paste, 12
  amaretti, 214
  iced praline torte, 180
  macaroons, 233
  tapas of olives, cheese and, 122
amaretti, 214
Amaretto mousses with Chocolate
  Sauce, 186
anchovy spread, 149
apples: apple and mint jelly, 155
  apple and nut stuffing, 36
  crab, apple and lavender jelly, 154
  crunchy apple and almond flan, 170
  filo crackers, 134
apricots: apricot and orange stuffing,
  142
  apricot and raisin stuffing, 140
  golden ginger compote, 162
avocados: celery, avocado and walnut
  salad, 116
  guacamole, 124

B

beef: Chateaubriand with béarnaise
  sauce, 49
  filet mignon with mushrooms, 48
  fillet of beef with ratatouille, 98
  hot salt beef on a stick, 127
  roast beef with roasted sweet
    peppers, 50
biscuits: amaretti, 214
  cheeselets, 120
  chocolate kisses, 211
  Christmas biscuits, 208
  cocktail biscuits, 121
  festive gingerbread, 196
  ginger Florentines, 210
  Hogmanay shortbread, 207
  macaroons, 233
  mocha Viennese swirls, 215
  orange shortbread fingers, 206
  sablés with goat's cheese and
    strawberries, 136
  striped biscuits, 232
black buns, mini, 235
blinis with smoked salmon and dill
  cream, 131
brandy: brandied eggnog, 244
  brandy Alexander, 247
  plum brandy, 251

poached spiced plums in brandy, 156
bread: bread sauce, 143
  stollen, 201
Brie and walnuts, grilled, 25
Brussels sprouts: festive, 78
  stir-fried Brussels sprouts, 85
Buck's fizz (mimosa), 246
bulgur wheat and ham salad, 115
butter: Cumberland rum butter, 147
  savoury butters, 148

C

cake tins, lining, 13
cakes: chocolate and chestnut Yule log,
  176
  individual Dundee cakes, 234
  light jewelled fruit cake, 202
  mini black buns, 235
  moist and rich Christmas cake, 204
  nut and glacé fruit ring, 199
  panettone, 200
  spiced Christmas cake, 203
candle ring, Advent, 9
caramel: iced praline torte, 180
carrots: carrot and coriander soup, 16
  carrot, apple and orange coleslaw,
    117
  glazed carrots with cider, 84
carving turkey, 12
celery, avocado and walnut salad, 116
champagne: buck's fizz (mimosa), 246
Chateaubriand with béarnaise sauce, 49
cheese: cheese and spinach flan, 70
  cheese, rice and vegetable strudel, 66
  cheeselets, 120
  cocktail biscuits, 121
  goat's cheese soufflé, 24
  grilled Brie and walnuts, 25
  Parmesan filo triangles, 132
  Roquefort and cucumber mousse, 26
  Roquefort tartlets, 33
  sablés with goat's cheese and
    strawberries, 136
  vegetable crumble with anchovies, 68
  vegetable gnocchi, 64
  vegetarian Christmas pie, 62
cheesecake, raspberry and white
chocolate, 190
chestnuts: chestnut and mushroom loaf,
  71
  chestnut stuffing, 140
chicken: chicken roll, 103

chicken satay with peanut sauce, 129
  chicken with morels, 43
  chicken with red wine vinegar, 42
  farmhouse pâté, 31
chocolate: Amaretto mousses with
  chocolate sauce, 186
  chocolate and chestnut Yule log, 176
  chocolate crêpes with plums and
    port, 188
  chocolate, date and almond filo coil,
    189
  chocolate kisses, 211
  chocolate roulade with coconut
    cream, 192
  chocolate sorbet with red fruits, 184
  chocolate truffles, 227
  fruit fondant chocolates, 226
  ginger Florentines, 210
  Irish chocolate velvet, 245
  mocha Viennese swirls, 215
  orange, mint and coffee meringues,
    223
  peppermint chocolate sticks, 230
  raspberry and white chocolate
    cheesecake, 190
  rich chocolate and fruit fondue, 137
  tiramisu in chocolate cups, 179
  truffle Christmas puddings, 231
chorizo puffs, pastry-wrapped, 126
Christmas biscuits, 208
Christmas cakes, 203-4
Christmas chutney, 150
Christmas cranberry bombe, 183
Christmas pie, vegetarian, 62
Christmas pudding, Traditional, 174
Christmas salad, 22
Christmas spirit, 250
Christmas tree, everlasting, 9
chutneys, 150–2
cinnamon rolls, 213
citrus whisky, 251
claret, mulled, 243
cocktail biscuits, 121
coffee: mocha Viennese swirls, 215
  tiramisu in chocolate cups, 179
coleslaw, carrot, apple and orange, 117
consommé, oriental duck, 19
couscous, spiced vegetable, 72
crab-apple and lavender jelly, 154
crackers, filo, 134
cranberries: Christmas cranberry
  bombe, 183

Christmas spirit, 250
cranberry and rice stuffing, 140
cranberry frost, 242
cranberry kiss, 248
cranberry sauce, 143
crème Anglais, 146
crêpes: chocolate, 188
  with orange sauce, 166
cucumber and Roquefort mousse, 26
Cumberland rum butter, 147
Cumberland sauce, baked gammon
    with, 52
custard: baked custard with burnt
    sugar, 182
  crème Anglais, 146

D
date-filled pastries, 212
drinks, 242–51
duck: duck with orange sauce, 44
  oriental duck consommé, 19
Dundee cakes, individual, 234

E
eggnog, brandied, 244
eggs: baked eggs with creamy leeks, 32
evergreen garland, 8

F
farmhouse pâté, 31
filo crackers, 134
filo vegetable pie, 74
foie gras pâté in filo cups, 28
fondant icing, 13
fondue, rich chocolate and fruit, 137
French beans with bacon and cream,
    87
fruit: Christmas chutney, 150
  fruit and ginger ale, 249
  fruit fondant chocolates, 226
  fruits in liqueurs, 239
  glacé fruits, 225
  marzipan fruits, 229
  rich chocolate and fruit fondue, 137
  ruby fruit salad, 161
  sea bass with citrus fruit, 54
fudge, creamy, 222

G
game terrine, 94
gammon, baked with Cumberland
    sauce, 52

garland, evergreen, 8
gin, fruit, 251
ginger: festive gingerbread, 196
  fruit and ginger ale, 249
  ginger Florentines, 210
  ginger trifle, 160
  gingerbread heart ring, 198
  golden ginger compote, 162
glacé fruits, 225
gnocchi, 64, 76
goat's cheese soufflé, 24
goose, roast with caramelized apples,
    36
gougère, vegetable, 65
Grand Marnier soufflés, frozen, 178
gratin Dauphinois, 88
guacamole, 124

H
ham and bulgur wheat salad, 115
Hasselback potatoes, 91
Hogmanay shortbread, 207

I
ice cream: Christmas cranberry bombe,
    183
iced praline torte, 180
icings, 13
Irish chocolate velvet, 245

J
jellies, 154–5

K
koulibiac, 66
kumquats: golden ginger compote, 162

L
lamb: lamb tikka, 128
  roast stuffed lamb, 51
leeks: baked eggs with creamy leeks,
    32
  leek and onion tart, 80
  mini leek and onion tartlets, 104
liqueurs: festive liqueurs, 251
  fruits in liqueurs, 239
liver: chicken liver mousse, 30
  farmhouse pâté, 31
lobster thermidor, 58

M
macaroons, 233

mango and amaretti strudel, 172
marshmallows, 228
marzipan fruits, 229
meringues, orange, mint and coffee,
    223
millefeuille, mini, 168
mimosa, 246
mincemeat: almond mincemeat tartlets,
    217
  de luxe mincemeat tart, 218
  double-crust mince pies, 216
mocha Viennese swirls, 215
mousseline sauce, 145
mousses: Amaretto, 186
  chicken liver, 30
  Roquefort and cucumber, 26
mulled claret, 243
mushrooms: chestnut and mushroom
    loaf, 71
  chicken with morels, 43
  cream of mushroom soup, 17
  filet mignon with mushrooms, 48
  vegetarian Christmas pie, 62
  wild mushroom tart, 100
  wild mushroom polenta, 23
mussels, sole with prawns and, 56

N
nut and glacé fruit ring, 199

O
onions: onion marmalade, 30
  thyme-roasted onions, 81
orange: Buck's fizz (mimosa), 246
  crêpes with orange sauce, 166
  duck with orange sauce, 44
  orange, mint and coffee meringues,
    223
  orange shortbread fingers, 206

P
panettone, 200
Parmesan filo triangles, 132
parsley, lemon and thyme stuffing, 142
parsnip and chestnut croquettes, 83
pâtés, 28, 31
peaches stuffed with mascarpone
    cream, 164
pears: spiced pears in red wine, 163
  spiced pickled pears, 157
peas with baby onions and cream, 86
peppermint chocolate sticks, 230

peppers: peppers in olive oil, 237
  roast beef with roasted sweet
    peppers, 50
pheasant: roast pheasant with port, 40
piccalilli, 151
pies: double-crust mince pies, 216
  filo vegetable pie, 74
  turkey and cranberry pie, 96
  vegetarian Christmas pie, 62
pilaff, smoked trout, 110
pizza wedges, spicy sun-dried tomato,
  130
plums: chocolate crêpes with, 188
  plum brandy, 251
  poached spiced plums in brandy, 156
pork: tenderloin wrapped in bacon, 53
potatoes: gratin Dauphinois, 88
  Hasselback potatoes, 91
  mini filled jacket potatoes, 133
  sautéed potatoes, 90
praline: iced praline torte, 180
prawns: prawn toasts, 125
  sole with prawns and mussels, 56
  warm prawn salad with spicy
    marinade, 20
preserve, fresh fruit, 238
pumpkin: pumpkin gnocchi, 76
  pumpkin soup, 18

Q
quince paste, 153

R
raisin and nut stuffing, 142
raspberries: fresh fruit preserve, 238
  mini millefeuille, 168
  raspberry and white chocolate
    cheesecake, 190
ratatouille, fillet of beef with, 98
red cabbage, sweet and sour, 82
redcurrant jelly: baked gammon with
  Cumberland sauce, 52
red fruit filo baskets, 169
rice: cheese, rice and vegetable strudel,
  66
  cranberry and rice stuffing, 140
  smoked trout pilaff, 110
  turkey rice salad, 114
roasting times, turkey, 12
Roquefort and cucumber mousse, 26
Roquefort tartlets, 33
royal icing, 13

ruby fruit salad, 161
rum butter, Cumberland, 147

S
sablés with goat's cheese and
  strawberries, 136
salads, 20–2, 114–17
salmon: classic whole salmon, 106
  layered salmon terrine, 108
  salmon steaks with sorrel sauce, 59
sauces: bread, 143
  cranberry, 143
  crème Anglais, 146
  mousseline, 145
  tartare, 144
sea bass with citrus fruit, 54
shortbread, 206–7
smoked salmon: blinis with dill cream
  and, 131
  smoked salmon salad, 21
smoked trout pilaff, 110
sole with prawns and mussels, 56
sorbet, chocolate, 184
soufflés: frozen Grand Marnier, 178
  goat's cheese, 24
soups, 16–19
spinach: cheese and spinach flan, 70
  creamy spinach purée, 79
  roast stuffed lamb, 51
  vegetable gnocchi, 64
stollen, 201
striped biscuits, 232
strudels, 66, 172
stuffings: apple and nut, 36
  apricot and orange, 142
  apricot and raisin, 140
  chestnut, 140
  cranberry and rice, 140
  parsley, lemon and thyme, 142
  prune, 53
  raisin and nut, 142
sweet and sour red cabbage, 82
sweets, 222–30

T
tapas of almonds, olives and cheese,
  122
tartare sauce, 144
tarts: almond mincemeat tartlets, 217
  cheese and spinach flan, 70
  crunchy apple and almond flan, 170
  de luxe mincemeat tart, 218

  leek and onion tart, 80
  mini leek and onion tartlets, 104
  Roquefort tartlets, 33
  tomato and basil tart, 112
  wild mushroom tart, 100
terrines: game, 94
  garden vegetable, 102
  layered salmon, 108
tiramisu in chocolate cups, 179
tomatoes: spicy sun-dried tomato pizza
  wedges, 130
  tomato and basil tart, 112
  tomato chutney, 152
trifle, ginger, 160
trout, smoked see smoked trout
truffles: chocolate truffles, 227
  truffle Christmas puddings, 231
turkey: carving, 12
  roast turkey, 12, 38
  turkey and cranberry pie, 96
  turkey rice salad, 114
Turkish delight, 224
twig heart door wreath, 8

V
vegetables: cheese, rice and vegetable
  strudel, 66
  fillet of beef with ratatouille, 98
  filo vegetable pie, 74
  garden vegetable terrine, 102
  piccalilli, 151
  spiced vegetable couscous, 72
  vegetable crumble with anchovies, 68
  vegetable gnocchi, 64
  vegetable gougère, 65
vegetarian Christmas pie, 62
venison, roast leg of, 46
Viennese swirls, mocha, 215
vinegars, flavoured, 236
vodka: Christmas spirit, 250

W
whisky: citrus whisky, 251
  Irish chocolate velvet, 245
wild mushroom tart, 100
wine: mulled claret, 243
  spiced pears in red wine, 163
wreath, twig heart door, 8

Y
Yule log, chocolate and chestnut, 176